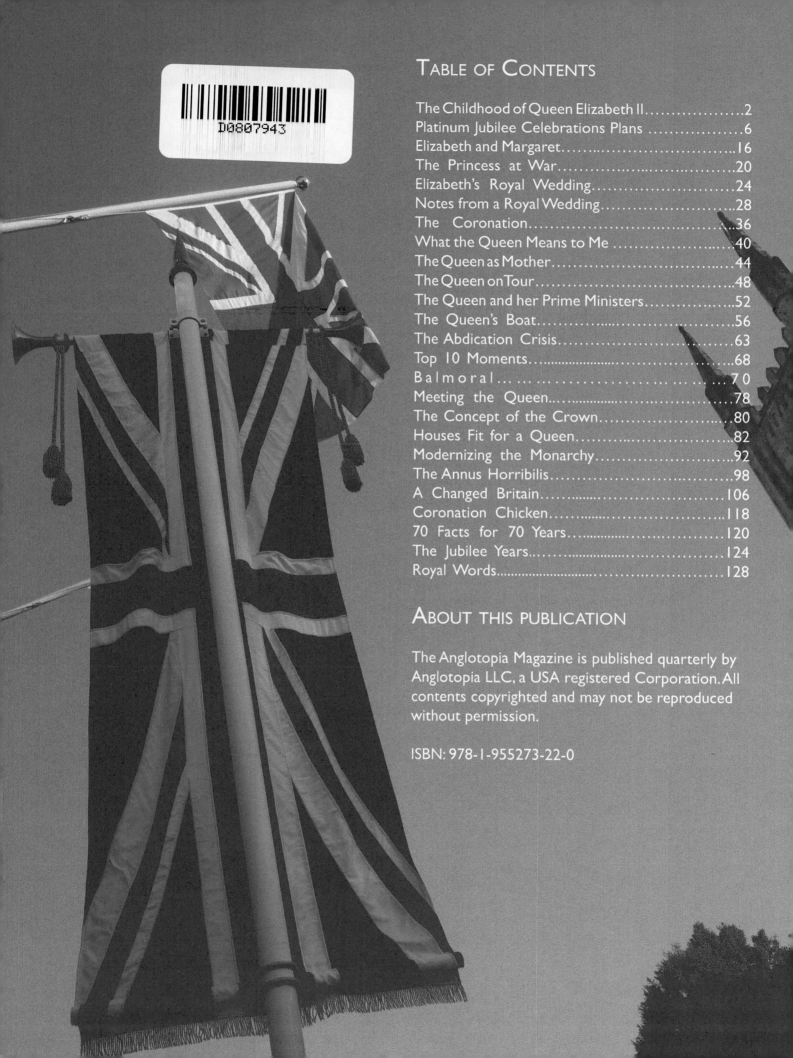

Table of Contents

The Childhood of Queen Elizabeth II....................2
Platinum Jubilee Celebrations Plans 6
Elizabeth and Margaret...............................16
The Princess at War...................................20
Elizabeth's Royal Wedding..........................24
Notes from a Royal Wedding.......................28
The Coronation......................................36
What the Queen Means to Me 40
The Queen as Mother.................................44
The Queen on Tour....................................48
The Queen and her Prime Ministers...............52
The Queen's Boat....................................56
The Abdication Crisis...............................63
Top 10 Moments.....................................68
Balmoral...70
Meeting the Queen...................................78
The Concept of the Crown.........................80
Houses Fit for a Queen.............................82
Modernizing the Monarchy........................92
The Annus Horribilis................................98
A Changed Britain..................................106
Coronation Chicken................................118
70 Facts for 70 Years..............................120
The Jubilee Years...................................124
Royal Words...128

About this Publication

The Anglotopia Magazine is published quarterly by Anglotopia LLC, a USA registered Corporation. All contents copyrighted and may not be reproduced without permission.

ISBN: 978-1-955273-22-0

THE PRINCESS

THE CHILDHOOD OF QUEEN ELIZABETH II

It might seem surprising to us today to think that Queen Elizabeth II hasn't always been Queen Elizabeth II; she is, after all, the longest-reigning British monarch in history, as well as the Western world's longest-serving leader. We sometimes picture her like the birth of Athena, springing from Zeus's head fully grown and in full battle regalia. But of course, she wasn't born queen or even heir to the throne. Her father was Albert, Duke of York, King George V's second son. It was Uncle David, momentarily (for 10 months, anyway) reigning as King Edward VIII, who was meant to be king.

Perhaps it was exactly because she was not meant to be a queen that she was able to have such a charmed, happy childhood. Elizabeth Alexandra Mary Windsor was born in London on 21 April 1926. Just as with Britain's royals today, her birth was met with a media firestorm, proving that even if she wasn't yet the "heiress presumptive," she was still not just a normal little girl. In fact, her future first Prime Minister Winston Churchill visited the family in Scotland at Balmoral when Elizabeth was just two years old and was completely taken by her charm. He called her "a character" and someone with "an air of authority."

Even before her father took the throne in 1936 when Elizabeth was just age 10, young Lilibet, as she was called, had developed quite a personality. She was said to be shy and humble, yet clever, astute, witty, precise, and cheerful. In 1927, when Elizabeth was still just a toddler, her parents went on a royal tour of New Zealand and Australia, leaving their daughter with King George V and Queen Mary (and presumably a host of nannies and staff). Her grandmother, Queen Mary, called her "a joy." Lilibet had already stolen her grandparents' hearts. Her grandfather, King George V, who was rather harsh with his own sons, was crazy about Lilibet. She clearly was just as crazy about him, calling him Grandpa England. With the birth of little sister Margaret in 1930, four years after Elizabeth, the family was complete and happy.

Margaret and Elizabeth seemed to be a good complement to each other. While Elizabeth was dignified and standoffish, Margaret was lively and fun, often playing practical jokes on the staff (picture the von Trapp children putting frogs in Frauline Maria's pockets) while Elizabeth watched and giggled. In public occasions, Elizabeth was clearly already the older sister more ready for

monarchy, at one point telling Margaret before an outing, "If you see someone with a silly hat, Margaret, you must not point at it and laugh."2 And yet they were good friends and had a lot of fun together. Of course, there were not a lot of other options, since they did not leave to go to school or make friends with outsiders. One of Lilibet's favorite playmates was her Uncle David, in the years before his abdication when the whole relationship went sour. He often came to play in the family's after-supper games; he even gave the young princess her first copy of Winnie-the-Pooh, which was published the same year as her birth. Elizabeth's father, and soon the rest of their little family, called each other "we four," and had a strong bond of friendship and fun, probably realizing that they were really the only ones who know what it was like to be a family like they were. The press loved them.

Besides parlor games with the family, Lilibet loved her horses. She started riding at age three and took to it immediately, a love she has kept throughout her life. It was her father who taught her all about breeding and racing; she loved to ride and explore the stables with him at their estate in Norfolk—Sandringham—and at Hampton Court and Balmoral. When she wasn't outside with the horses, she was often inside with her pile of toy ponies, brushing their hair and arranging them on the stairs, sometimes even pretending to be a pony herself and refusing to answer those around her: "I couldn't answer you as a pony."3 It was also her father who gave her her first Welsh Corgi, what was to become her signature breed. They named the dog Duke of York, calling him "Dookie" (again with the nicknames); after that, she was never without at least one dog, sometimes many underfoot. She even took her dog Susan on her honeymoon with Prince Philip.

In 1932, the family brought in a lively Scottish nanny, Marion Crawford, affectionately known as Crawfie (this family likes their nicknames). In an effort to introduce the young princesses to life outside the "glass curtain," as she called it, Crawfie would take the girls into town on the bus and the tube in the years before the abdication. After the abdication, when it became clear that Elizabeth was not going to do as much traipsing around London, Crawfie arranged for a troop of Girl Guides (think British Girl Scouts) to meet at Buckingham Palace as a way to help Elizabeth make friends and have

a normal (or normal-ish) childhood. This was not your average group of Girl Guides, of course, no Eastenders in the mix, but 20 girls of about Margaret and Elizabeth's ages carefully chosen from their relatives, of which there were so many, and local aristocrats. Still, the young princesses got to run around exploring the 40 acres of gardens at the palace, making campfires and learning outdoor skills. Crawfie and her young charges were very fond of each other, and they were together for years. However, in 1949 the nanny wrote a (very sweet, kindly, completely innocuous) memoir of her time with Elizabeth and Margaret, and the family cut her out completely for such a show of disloyalty, prompting the Queen Mother to cry, "We can only think that our late and completely trusted governess has gone off her head." 4

Before Crawfie's abrupt departure from the family, she also acted as tutor to the two girls. In the years before King George VI's succession, Elizabeth's education was fairly relaxed. She was expected to learn language and history, but no math or government to speak of. Crawfie remembers the first book she read with Lilibet and Margaret—"Peter Pan in Kensington Gardens", an appropriate choice as it was written and took place just down the street. Marion Crawford was also expected to teach her manners and penmanship, as well, skills that would be useful to a life of royalty but nothing to prepare her for the monarchy. Elizabeth's mother, Elizabeth Duchess of York, had taught Lilibet to read herself, often reading aloud to her. It was the Duchess of York who encouraged a light education, often interrupting her studying hours for little outings, and one day bringing home a stack of 18 P.G. Wodehouse novels, hardly heavy reading. Still, it was also the Duchess of York who taught Lilibet religion. Lilibet grew up with a strong Christian faith, learning her Psalms and reading the Book of Common Prayer with her mother. This turned out to be a great asset later on when she became head of the Church of England, hardly something her mother could have expected as they were saying their prayers together before bed.

The Windsors were a dutiful family, instilling that sense of duty in Elizabeth from a young age. Queen Mary was particularly stiff-upper-lip about royal duties, teaching Lilibet how to walk and sit up straight so as not to embarrass herself—traditional royal family skills. Lilibet learned the useful skill of keeping a diary from her mother. When complimented on her daily writings in later years, the Queen said, "It's not really a diary-like Queen Victoria's . . . or as detailed as that. It's quite small." She called it just a habit, "like scrubbing your teeth."5 Despite her humility about it, we can imagine that one day beyond her death, those daily entries will be quite enlightening to the rest of us. The Duchess of York, by now Queen Elizabeth herself, was also a great example to Lilibet of how to treat other people, a characteristic that Lilibet has hung onto throughout her life and reign. Her mother told her, "if you find something or somebody a bore, the fault lies in you."6 Now there's a quality more of us could use in our modern lives, and those who know Queen Elizabeth II often comment on how interested she is in people, relating to them in a way that might seem surprising considering her sheltered upbringing. The family also tried to teach Lilibet and Margaret frugality and money management, giving the girls an allowance of five shillings a week—a somewhat comical idea to us today, considering Lilibet already had a yearly allowance of 6,000 pounds, and where was she really going to spend her weekly allowance anyway?

Young Elizabeth's easy, simplified education changed dramatically in 1936 when her father reluctantly took the throne, and she became the heiress presumptive ("presumptive" just in case her parents had a son, but of course they didn't). Suddenly Elizabeth needed to learn all sorts of new things—maybe not math, which was never her strong suit, but government and more history and languages, to be sure. To that end, in 1939 the family brought in Sir Henry Marten, vice-provost of nearby Eton College (nearby when they were at Windsor, that is, but they were in Windsor quite often, causing the queen to call Windsor her home). Marten was very knowledgeable as a professor at Eton, we might think of him as stuffy and a bit of a bore, but for Lilibet, he was engaging and brought history alive. That was, of course, just what she needed in the years of royal tutelage she had ahead of her. Marten taught her the ins and outs of the British Constitution with some instruction in American history, as well. As Americans we consider our constitution to be fairly straightforward as a document that was, for the most part, written all in one go. The British Constitution, however, is more of a conglomeration of accumulated laws and precedents, not surprising considering their history is well more than 1,000 years older than that of the United States and has gone through numerous governmental and monarchical permutations. The King's private secretary, and later Elizabeth's, Tommy Lascelles instructed Marten to "hide nothing" about the constitution and how to navigate it. Marten clearly took this task to heart—Elizabeth's Prime Ministers were often impressed with her command of the Constitution and her knowledge of the workings of Parliament, they were perhaps even surprised by her detailed knowledge. Marten also taught her critical thinking and how to use her best judgment in assessing an argument, a skill that would benefit her throughout her reign.

Along with learning the intricacies of the British government, Elizabeth's family brought in a French tutor for the young princesses, a Belgian vicomtesse with the improbable name of Marie-Antoinette de Bellaigue. They called her Toni (again with the nicknames, but these names are all such a mouthful, who can blame them?). Lilibet learned to speak fluently, a great skill in her future as Queen, never needing an interpreter in France and her other francophone territories. Her family and advisers clearly had quite a lot of foresight and experience in choosing her education and her educators, her natural curiosity and intelligence helped her to adapt well to the education she suddenly found herself needing.

These formative years were, perhaps surprisingly, happy and loving for the future queen. While the Queen refuses to grant interviews, she talks very fondly of her childhood and her years as "we four." She still has in her near future a world war, a marriage, the death of her father, and her own reign. It seems like it would be almost impossible to prepare for all the things she would see in her life, yet she seemed perfectly positioned to take them all on with the consistency, discipline, wit, and intelligence she learned from the start.

A PARTY FIT FOR A QUEEN
GUIDE TO THE PLATINUM JUBILEE CELEBRATIONS
BY LAURA PORTER

In 2022, Her Majesty The Queen became the first British monarch to celebrate a Platinum Jubilee. Queen Elizabeth II acceded to the throne on 6th February 1952 when just 25 years old and has given an incredible seventy years of service.

Throughout this year there are Platinum Jubilee celebrations across the United Kingdom to celebrate The Queen's historic reign. Such events help reinforce the Sovereign's role as a focus for national identity and unity as people across the Commonwealth come together to mark an important occasion for their Head of State.

Members of the Royal Family are travelling around the country to undertake a variety of engagements to mark this historic occasion culminating with the focal point of the Platinum Jubilee Weekend in June 2022.

Even though February was the official anniversary marking the Queen's 70-year reign, as with the Queen's Golden and Diamond Jubilees, the first week in June has been chosen for the celebratory weekend, with the summer offering a better chance of good weather.

The Queen will be 96 at the time of the Platinum Jubilee events. Her real birthday is on 21 April but we celebrate her official birthday in June. 2022 is set to be a blockbuster year, bursting with national pride and showcasing the best of Britain to the world.

Extra Bank Holiday

We usually have a public holiday on the last Monday of June for Whitsun (Pentecost) but that has moved for 2022 and we have gained an extra day off. Instead of the Monday, we've got a Spring Bank Holiday on Thursday 2nd June and the extra day is Friday 3rd June for the Platinum Jubilee Bank Holiday.

This four-day Jubilee weekend will provide an opportunity for people to come together to celebrate the historic milestone. There are lots of public events planned as well as national moments of reflection on the Queen's 70 years of service.

What Is Planned?

The official commemorations are being arranged jointly with The Royal Household and the Department for Digital, Culture, Media and Sport. The four-day celebrations will reflect on Her Majesty's reign and her impact on the UK and the world since 1952. This historic event will feature an extensive programme that combines the best of British ceremonial splendour and pageantry with cutting edge artistic and technological displays. We are being promised a spectacular weekend of celebrations for a truly historic moment that deserves a celebration to remember. To aid community celebrations in England and Wales, pubs, clubs and bars could be allowed to stay open for an extra two hours over the bank holiday weekend.

It is not clear which events the Queen will attend or take part in as she was ordered to rest by doctors in October 2021 following an overnight hospital stay for unspecified preliminary investigations, and she tested positive for Covid-19 in February 2022. The bulk of the Jubilee duties is thought likely to be given to the rest of the royal family, including the Prince of Wales and Duchess of Cornwall.

The Queen usually spends the anniversary of her accession privately at Sandringham. Sandringham and Balmoral will both be open for residents and visitors to enjoy the celebrations across the long weekend. At Sandringham, local residents can watch 'Platinum Party at the Palace' on the big screen in the Royal Parkland.

January: Platinum Pudding Competition

The official Jubilee celebrations began on 10th January 2022 when Fortnum & Mason launched the Platinum Pudding Competition to find a dish to dedicate to the Queen's 70 years on the throne. Recipes will be judged by an expert panel, including Dame Mary Berry.

April: Severn Valley Railway

Severn Valley Railway is painting its 34027 Taw Valley engine in regal purple and temporarily renaming it 'Elizabeth II'. The engine will be painted by April

and will be restored to its original green after a few months.

May: Royal Windsor Horse Show

From 12th to 15th May 2022, more than 500 horses and 1,000 performers will take part in a 90-minute show called A Gallop Through History taking the Windsor Castle audience from Elizabeth I to the present day.

May: St Paul's Cathedral

From 25th May to December 2022, St Paul's Cathedral has a display called The Monarch and the Changing World that explores the grand ceremonial occasions held at the Cathedral to commemorate the Royal Jubilees of four British monarchs: George III, Victoria, George V and Elizabeth II.

THURSDAY 2ND JUNE 2022

The Queen's Birthday Parade (Trooping the Colour): This event usually takes place on the second Saturday of June to mark the Queen's official birthday but for 2022 it will be on Thursday 2nd June to start the long weekend of celebrations. The colour will be trooped on Horse Guards Parade by the 1st Battalion, Irish Guards, and over 1,200 officers and soldiers from the Household Division who will put on a display.

The Parade begins at Buckingham Palace and travels down The Mall to Horse Guard's Parade to arrive at 11 am. Trooping of the Colour is the official inspection of the guards and then the Royal Family travel back to the Palace to watch the traditional RAF fly-past from the Buckingham Palace balcony at 1 pm.

Platinum Jubilee Beacons: The United Kingdom's long tradition of celebrating Royal Jubilees, weddings and coronations with the lighting of beacons will be continued to mark the Platinum Jubilee.

More than 1,500 beacons will be lit throughout the United Kingdom, the Channel Islands, Isle of Man and UK Overseas Territories at the same time as

the principal beacon at Buckingham Palace. For the first time, beacons will also be lit in each of the capital cities of the Commonwealth countries as well.

God Save The Queen: Choir of the Earth is presenting the Her Majesty with a new recording of God Save The Queen performed by volunteers from across the world. Rehearsals took place in March and an online concert performance is happening on Thursday 2nd June 2022 to hear all the voices combined for the first time.

FRIDAY 3RD JUNE 2022

Service of Thanksgiving: A Service of Thanksgiving for The Queen's reign will be held at St Paul's Cathedral.

SATURDAY 4TH JUNE 2022

The Derby at Epsom Downs: Her Majesty The Queen, accompanied by members of the Royal Family, will attend the Cazoo Derby at Epsom

Downs in Surrey. It is Britain's richest flat horse race. Her Majesty has long enjoyed the thrill of horse racing and she owns many thoroughbred horses for use in racing.

Platinum Party at the Palace: In the evening, the BBC will stage and broadcast a special live concert from Buckingham Palace. Some of the world's greatest entertainers are billed to perform at the concert to celebrate the most significant moments from the Queen's reign. UK residents can apply to attend this special event via a ballot.

SUNDAY 5TH JUNE 2022

The Big Jubilee Lunch: The annual Big Lunch began in 2009 to encourage communities to celebrate their connections and get to know each other better. In 2022 The Big Lunch is inviting friends and neighbours to share food and fun as part of the Platinum Jubilee celebrations so we can expect to see plenty of street parties.

The Platinum Jubilee Pageant: This event will round

off four days of public celebrations telling the story of The Queen's long reign and our transforming society. The carnival-style pageant featuring more than 5,000 people from across the United Kingdom and the Commonwealth, includes a trapeze artist suspended beneath a huge helium balloon.

The procession, which is in three acts, will travel through the streets of Westminster and along the Mall past Buckingham Palace. Schoolchildren across the country have been invited to create a picture of their hopes for the planet over the next 70 years, and some of their designs will be put onto the 200 silk flags that create a River of Hope.

The first act is a military spectacle with marching bands and the second act will tell the story of the Queen's reign and how society has transformed throughout the decades. An original story by writer Sir Michael Morpurgo called 'There Once is a Queen' will be brought to life and the parade will feature music, dance and impressive puppets such as colossal 'Queen's Beasts' the height of three-storey houses and dragons with the dimension of London buses. The third act, the finale of the grand celebrations of the Pageant, will be revealed nearer the time.

The organisers tell us, it is no coincidence that the Platinum Jubilee Pageant falls on World Environment Day on 5th June 2022. Sustainability will be considered throughout the planning of the Pageant.

Platinum Jubilee 70K Ultra

This event in Portsmouth is encouraging runners to run for up to 70k on the day or just do one lap and complete 24k. Multi-sport triathletes can choose to run, cycle, kayak or a combination, and all who reach the finish line will receive a Jubilee medal.

Classic Car Run: The Rotary Club of Bodmin has a classic car run planned with 70 cars – one for each year of The Queen's reign. The British-only vehicles will be travelling 70 miles from Bodmin to Penzance in Cornwall.

July: The Royal Collection Trust

From July, three displays marking the Queen's accession to the throne, the Coronation and Jubilees will be put on at official royal residences: Buckingham Palace, Windsor Castle and the Palace of Holyroodhouse. The Queen's portraits taken by photographer Dorothy Wilding between 1953 and 1956, personal jewellery worn for sittings, and carriages will be on display at the Summer Opening at Buckingham Palace. At Windsor Castle, the Coronation Dress and Robe of Estate worn by The Queen for her Coronation at Westminster Abbey on 2nd June 1953 will be shown to visitors. The Palace of Holyroodhouse will display the outfits worn by the Queen for her Silver, Golden and Diamond Jubilees.

Superbloom at the Tower of London

Superbloom is a Commonwealth-themed garden in the historic moat of the Tower of London. During spring 2022, over 20 million seeds are being sown in the moat establishing the first stage of a permanent transformation of the moat into a new natural landscape in the heart of the City of London. Open from 1 June to 18 September 2022, visitors can wander along a weaving path into the centre of the flowers accompanied by a specially-commissioned sound installation and sculptural elements. Upon arrival, visitors can grab a mat and take the Superbloom slide down to the moat or choose the more conventional fully-accessible entrance.

The Queen's Green Canopy

Launched in May 2021, people across the United Kingdom have been encouraged to 'Plant a Tree for the Jubilee'. This unique tree-planting initiative, created to mark Her Majesty's Platinum Jubilee, is to help the environment and make local areas greener by planting trees from October 2021, when the tree planting season begins, through to the end of the Jubilee year in 2022. The idea is to create a legacy in honour of The Queen which will benefit future generations.

As well as inviting the planting of new trees, The Queen's Green Canopy will dedicate a network of 70 Ancient Woodlands across the United Kingdom and identify 70 Ancient Trees to celebrate Her Majesty's 70 years of service.

Jubilee Emblem

The Royal Household in partnership with the Victoria and Albert Museum (V&A) invited young people aged 13 – 25 to design an emblem for The Queen's Platinum Jubilee in 2022.

The chosen emblem design is based on an original illustration drawn by Edward Roberts, a 19-year-old student at the University of Leeds. The emblem features a purple and platinum design. The continuous platinum line reveals a stylised St Edward's Crown, incorporating the number 70, on a round purple background associated with royalty and signifying a royal seal. The elegant font Perpetua, meaning forever, is an acknowledgement to the first British Monarch ever to mark 70 years on the throne.

Jubilee Medal

In keeping with tradition, a Platinum Jubilee medal will be awarded to people who work in public service including representatives of the Armed Forces, the emergency services and the prison services. This tradition stretches back to the reign of Queen Victoria when an official medal was designed to mark her 50th anniversary on the throne.

Royal Jubilees

Few British Monarchs have achieved reigns of 50 years. Henry III, Edward III and James VI and I reached the 50-year milestones but there are no records of how it was celebrated. The first British monarch to mark 50 years on the throne in a significant way was George III, followed by Queen Victoria.

Queen Elizabeth II has had significant Jubilee

celebrations in 1977 (for her Silver Jubilee), 2002 (for her Golden Jubilee) and 2012 (for her Diamond Jubilee).

During the summer months in 1977, the Queen embarked on a large scale tour, having decided that she wished to mark her Jubilee by meeting as many of her people as possible. No other Sovereign had visited so much of Britain in the course of just three months. I remember the street parties, seeing the Queen on the news everywhere and a lot of flag-waving.

A packed programme of events took place in 2002 to celebrate fifty years of The Queen's reign. Six key Jubilee themes shaped events: Celebration, Community, Service, Past and future, Giving thanks and Commonwealth. The Queen and The Duke of Edinburgh undertook extensive tours of the Commonwealth and the UK.

2012 was a bumper year for national pride as we had the Diamond Jubilee plus the London 2012 Olympic and Paralympic Games. The Diamond Jubilee was marked with a spectacular central weekend and a series of regional tours. The Queen and The Duke of Edinburgh travelled as widely as possible across England, Scotland, Wales and Northern Ireland, visiting every region during 2012 whilst other members of the Royal Family visited all of the Commonwealth realms (countries where The Queen is Head of State) between them.

6th February 2017 marked 65 years since The Queen acceded to the throne, becoming the first British Monarch to mark their Sapphire Jubilee although I don't remember us having any national celebrations.

Souvenirs

The earliest known English commemorative items date from the Restoration of Charles II as king in 1660, followed by his Coronation in 1661 and wedding in 1662. You can be sure there will be plenty of souvenirs to mark the Platinum Jubilee including coins and stamps.

The Royal Mint has released two collectable coins

designed by John Bergdahl. The 50p coin shows the Queen on horseback and the £5 crown features a regal design centralised by the quartered shield of the Royal Arms. Both coins feature the portrait of the Queen designed by Jody Clark. And the Royal Mail has released eight new stamps featuring photographs of the Queen throughout her reign.

Commemorative coins are not intended for general use and are almost always collected in uncirculated mint condition. Special issue coins were first used to mark a Royal Jubilee with the Golden Jubilee of Queen Victoria in 1887. The first stamps associated with a royal event were those issued in 1887 although they were not intended as commemorative issues.

Ceramics have also proved popular for Jubilee souvenirs. Commemorative items survive in significant numbers from the reign of George III onwards, taking advantage of industrialised production methods such as transfer prints to produce affordable items including mugs, bowls, plaques, jugs and urns.

I think we can safely expect to find commemorative mugs and tea towels selling well throughout 2022. I'm still using my Golden Jubilee tea towel so I could do with a replacement.

Extra Information

Bhumibol Adulyadej was the most recent monarch to celebrate a Platinum Jubilee in 2016. Sadly, he died shortly after official celebrations in Thailand took place.

South Gloucestershire Council has suggested that the Severn Bridge be renamed in honour of The Queen's Platinum Jubilee.

As part of the Platinum Jubilee Civic Honours, the Queen will give several settlements city status. There have been applications from 39 locations including Blackburn in Lancashire, Colchester in Essex and Dumfries in Scotland.

A stone statue of the Queen at over 6 ft high is being sculpted on-site at York Minster in an empty

niche at the west front to a design chosen by the Queen. The sculpture will overlook a new public square, proposed for Duncombe Place, to be called the Queen Elizabeth Square.

In summer 2022, Imperial War Museum London has an exhibition of iconic and poignant photographs showcasing how the Queen's life has been touched by war and conflict, from meeting troops before D-Day to serving in the Auxiliary Territorial Service in 1945 and standing on the balcony of Buckingham Palace on VE Day.

And don't forget about The Queen's Diamond Jubilee Galleries at Westminster Abbey in the stunning 13th-century triforium. Opened in 2018, the galleries showcase artefacts spanning the Abbey's remarkable 1000-year history.

Watching in the USA

As with the Diamond Jubilee in 2012, you can expect the major US network to have coverage of all the major events. It's a good excuse for the networks, especially the morning shows, to send their key talent to Britain to cover it. However, for the best coverage, you can find that on the BBC or the BBC world News Channel. The special concert will likely be aired in primetime, probably on ABC as it was in 2012 - but it will be a delayed airing because of the time difference. As for what plans the networks have, nothing was concrete when we went to press.

Laura Porter writes AboutLondonLaura.com and contributes to many other publications while maintaining an impressive afternoon tea addiction. You can find Laura on Twitter and Instagram as @AboutLondon and on Facebook as @ AboutLondonLaura.

THE PRINCESSES

THE SISTERS: ELIZABETH AND MARGARET

"Lilibet is my pride, Margaret is my joy," said their father, King George VI. That's a pretty telling statement from someone who knew them so well. Elizabeth, older by four years, was organized, composed, and responsible from a young age. Margaret was fun, lively, and commanded attention. The girls' nanny, Marion Crawford, would sometimes ask for Margaret not to be invited to the same events as Elizabeth once they got older, just so Elizabeth would have a chance to shine. The sisters, however, got along remarkably well, their personalities complementing each other. As children, Margaret was the one playing pranks on the staff while Elizabeth watched and giggled from the sidelines, and when Elizabeth would get up during the night to organize and lay out her clothes for the next day, it was Margaret who would get her to take a deep breath and let it go. They showed fierce loyalty to one another throughout the years. In fact, Margaret said later in life, "I've only twice ever had a row with my sister."

Margaret was born in 1930 in Glamis Castle (of Macbeth fame), in Scotland—the first member of the royal family born in Scotland in 300 years. Since she was just four years younger than her older sister, they were educated together, at least until Elizabeth became heir presumptive and needed a more rigorous education. Margaret sometimes felt like she was a little shortchanged in her education as compared to her sister, but she was considered very intelligent and quick, as well as clever and witty.

While horses weren't her passion in quite the same way as they were with Lilibet, she was an accomplished rider, swimmer, and pianist. She was considered too young during World War II to serve as Elizabeth did, but that didn't shelter her from the learning experiences of the war, hiding in the bomb shelter under Windsor Castle and interacting with the Grenadier Guards. And she loved her fun with the Girl Guides, both at Buckingham Palace and in the war years at Windsor, getting dirty, making new friends, exploring the outdoors—in her older years and until her death she served as President and Chairman of the Council of the Girl Guides Association.

Royal Tours with her sister and parents were a great education as well, touring for the first time in 1947 around South Africa. They were a close, happy family, enjoying their time together as "we four." Her parents doted on Margaret in a way that they maybe didn't with Elizabeth. As much as their parents tried to treat them the same, they weren't the same and didn't have the same future ahead of them.

Margaret commented on their diverging paths when Elizabeth was crowned Queen in 1953: "I've lost my father, and I've lost my sister. She will be so busy. Our lives will change." While their lives did change, their relationship stayed much the same. Elizabeth did not like confrontation with anyone, but least of all her beloved sister. Like her parents had, and her mother still continued to do, Elizabeth tried to let her younger sister do her own thing without wanting to interfere much. That didn't work out quite as well when Margaret fell for her father's equerry, Peter Townsend.

Margaret first met Group Captain Peter Townsend when he started working for her father in 1944 when she was just fourteen years old—he was thirty but didn't pay her much notice yet. He had already been equerry (an official member of the royal family's household staff) for the previous King George and was a dashing, decorated war hero from the Battle of Britain serving in the Royal Air Force. More importantly, for this story anyway, he was married with two sons. With Townsend and Margaret running in the same close circles for so long, their romance didn't become evident to the family and staff until a trip to Balmoral in 1951.

By 1952 when King George VI died, Townsend was divorced and working for the new Queen Elizabeth, and he and Margaret were quite the item, although that was not yet evident to the press. Late that year, after Queen Elizabeth had taken the throne but before her coronation, Townsend told the Queen's secretary, Tommy Lascelles, that he and Margaret wanted to marry. Lascelles promptly took that message to the Queen for a serious discussion because, of course, it wasn't that simple.

According to the Royal Marriages Act of 1772, no member of the royal family who is in direct line for the throne (Margaret at this point was number three, after Elizabeth's children Charles and Anne), could marry without the sovereign's permission before the age of 25, and after age 25, they had to get the permission of the Privy Council then wait a year to be sure there were no objections. In 1952, Margaret was only 22, sixteen years younger than Townsend. Elizabeth was in a dilemma.

Even though Margaret seemed a long way from ascending the throne, if something happened to Elizabeth, her sister would act as regent for a child king (in this case, Charles), this was not something to be taken lightly. As sovereign, Elizabeth could give her permission for her sister to marry a divorced man if she wanted to, even though that was not how the royal family worked and traditionally divorced persons did not socialize with the Queen. As Head of the Church of England, however, Elizabeth could not approve the match, nor did she want to, she was very religious and very anti-divorce. Uncle David, now Duke of Windsor's abdication to marry the (scandalously) divorced Wallis Simpson was still fresh in everyone's minds, and no one was eager to relive an experience like that.

This marriage issue quickly became a topic of discussion for Prime Minister Winston Churchill, and senior members of Parliament. The consensus was that if something happened and Margaret became Queen, the children of Margaret and the divorced Townsend would then be heirs to the throne, and that was unacceptable. By this point, the press had caught on to the romance, making this a royal scandal. At Elizabeth's coronation, Margaret and Townsend were seen acting cozy, with her brushing lint off his lapel; the public was now paying attention, which meant the Queen had to tread lightly. Lascelles did all the communicating with Churchill and the press on the issue, seeming to leave Elizabeth out of it (she doesn't like confrontation, remember).

Pretty soon Lascelles and Churchill contrived to have Townsend re-assigned to a post in Brussels, with the hope that the romance would fizzle while he was gone. Margaret, however, was holding out for her 25th birthday when she could marry without her sister's permission. By the time Peter Townsend returned, Margaret is 25, and Anthony Eden is the new Prime Minister. Eden spends some time at Balmoral with Elizabeth and Philip discussing the matter, then returns to London and takes the matter to Parliament—would

Parliament support the marriage if the Queen and the Church of England opposed? Parliament said no, leaving Eden with the task of telling Margaret the bad news. Margaret's choice was to drop the marriage issue altogether or marry Townsend but renounce her status and standing, including her royal allowance and basically access to her family. As much as Margaret loved Peter, her royal family had been her identity since birth; she didn't know any other life. She finally issued a statement, saying, "I would like it to be known that I have decided not to marry Group Captain Peter Townsend. Mindful of the church's teaching that Christian marriage is indissoluble and conscious of my duty to the Commonwealth, I have resolved to put these considerations before any others." It was a heartbreaking decision for Margaret, with a lot of public support behind her. The Queen had tried to appear that she was staying out of it, partly for Margaret's sake and partly for the press, yet she was clearly in the know all along. Margaret decided to remain living at Clarence House in London with her mother.

Just a few years later, Margaret got word that Townsend was marrying a young Belgian woman. That seemed to be all the inspiration she needed to marry, herself. "I received a letter from Peter in the morning, and that evening I decided to marry Tony." Margaret married Antony Armstrong-Jones in 1960. Tony was charming, handsome, and sophisticated. While he wasn't royalty and had a bit of a reputation (I think we all remember that episode of The Crown, shield your eyes, kids), he was from an aristocratic family, he had not been married, and Elizabeth wanted to give Margaret what she wanted. Theirs was the first televised royal wedding, with 300 million people watching the lavish ceremony at Westminster Abbey. So that their children would have a title, Elizabeth made Tony Earl Snowdon. Now Lord Snowdon, Tony and Margaret had their first child, David, in 1961, and their daughter, Sarah, in 1964. The couple seemed to do alright for a little while, enjoying big parties together and (mostly Margaret) royal events. But by 1975 the couple had separated among rumors of numerous affairs on both sides. Elizabeth was aware of her sister's behavior, it was hard to avoid—on of the rumors was Margaret and Mick Jagger—but she wanted to let her sister manage her own life while hoping they would avoid divorce. The press really liked reporting on Margaret's scandals, so after a while, it was just too much to ignore. After some new photos of Margaret and her lover surfaced in Mustique, the Queen finally had to give them permission to divorce in 1978. After all the talk of divorce in the royal family earlier, this was a big deal, not just for Margaret and Tony but for the future of royal marriages. This divorce really paved the way for the future divorces of some of Elizabeth's children, along with starting to lift the stereotype of divorced people mixing with the royal family.

Margaret's troubles were far from over, however. While Elizabeth was always modest and humble, not wishing to draw attention to herself, sometimes even sneaking into the theatre after the curtain went up so as not to steal anyone's thunder, Margaret didn't see things the same way. She insisted on people addressing her by her full title and curtsying properly. She participated in fewer and fewer royal duties, causing some to wonder why she was getting such a generous royal allowance, although she kept up with a lot of charity work throughout her life. She was lively and witty, but also a heavy drinker and smoker, caustic, and messy. Elizabeth and her staff were often left smoothing ruffled feathers behind the scenes; her antics made her unpopular with the press and the public. At the age of 67, Margaret suffered a mild stroke; in the following years, she was often bedridden with numerous health problems. She died in 2002, the same year as the increasingly popular Queen Mum and just before celebrating the Queen's Golden Jubilee.

Some speculate that Margaret's life turned out to be so much harder than expected because she was always in her sister's shadow, but that seems to be a reality of Margaret's own making. Her disappointment over Peter Townsend surely had something to do with it. Yet until the end, Margaret and her sister were always close. Even when Margaret was causing trouble for the Queen and the Palace, they were loyal to each other, always defending each other to the press and talking to each other daily. Margaret very kindly remarked, after the crisis and trauma of Princess Diana's death, "You kindly arranged everybody's lives after the accident and made life tolerable for the two boys . . . there, always in command, was you, listening to everyone and deciding on all the issues. I just felt you were wonderful."

PRINCESS AT WAR

LIFE OF A PRINCESS IN WARTIME

When World War II started in September 1939, King George VI was still a new king with a young family; Winston Churchill was gearing up to bolster his nation in enduring the long war ("Never surrender!"); and the future Queen Elizabeth was just thirteen years old. Those years of war turned out to be some of her most formative years, teaching her more than she would ever have learned in peacetime, working harder than she thought possible, meeting people she would not have met otherwise, and facing grief and turmoil right alongside her country.

The war years must have seemed very uncertain for young Elizabeth. Sure, she was unlikely to lose everything she owned like some people in London, but when your family is dedicated to service to your country and your country's future is at stake, and your parents are in the thick of the danger, Lilibet had a lot to be concerned about. With the start of the war, the King and Queen were urged to send the two princesses off to Canada to keep them safe. This was not an unreasonable request—Hitler and his armies immediately proved aggressive and ruthless, kids all over Great Britain were being evacuated to safer locations. But the Queen was insistent that she would not be separated from her daughters or her husband, and since George VI wouldn't budge from London, they were all staying in the country. When war broke out, the family was in Balmoral for their summer holiday, although the King and Queen soon returned to London. It was in the Highlands of Scotland that young Elizabeth got her first glimpse of wartime deprivations. In what was probably her first service in wartime, Lilibet helped her mother host tea for women and children displaced by the war. This would prove to be a recurring theme for the future Queen during the war—as a young teenager herself she seemed the perfect one to minister to the children left behind or sent away.

In 1939 the family kept to their tradition of spending Christmas at the royal estate in Norfolk, Sandringham. But after that initial popping around the countryside, the family settled into what would be their home for the duration of the war. Elizabeth and Margaret would spend almost all of their war years just outside the city, in Windsor, while their parents would stay at Buckingham Palace a few miles away in London. Being a royal residence of considerable size, Windsor Castle was seen as a target for the German forces because Windsor was quickly fortified, fitted with barbed wire, anti-aircraft guns, bomb shelters, and black-out curtains. Fearing a land invasion, King George even removed the gems from the Imperial Crown and buried them in a cookie tin under one of the entrances to Windsor Castle, as well as removing the priceless artwork from the walls and sending it off to a more secluded and secure estate. Lilibet did her share of protecting Margaret, as well, remarking, "I don't think people should talk about battle and things in front of Margaret. We don't want to upset her." Lilibet clearly knew there was something to be worried about, especially after they spent their first night in the bomb shelter at Windsor. Crawfie, their beloved nanny and governess, describes it this way: "The shelter was in one of the dungeons, not a particularly inviting place anyway. There lingered about it always the memory of others who had probably been incarcerated there and left some of their unhappiness behind them. The atmosphere was gloomy, and there were beetles." They would spend many nights down there, although after that first time the staff did a little more clearing out the doom and gloom, making it seem a bit homier and less beetle-y.

Continuing her outreach to the children displaced by war, Elizabeth gave her first radio broadcast in 1940 on the BBC program Children's Hour, addressed to children evacuated overseas. At just age 14, she very sweetly and confidently reassures the children listening, giving them hope and comfort, speaking of "victory" and "when peace comes." In the end, we even hear little Margaret wish everyone "good night, children." The future queen seems warm and sympathetic; something people will compliment her on for years to come. (It's well worth a listen, try it here: www.huffingtonpost.co.uk/2015/09/08/the-queen-elizabeth-longest-reigning-first-speech-refugees_n_8103470.html)

Life at Windsor during the war wasn't always quite so heavy, however. Crawfie was there with them and wanted to bring some fun and distraction into the home. She arranged pantomimes for the young princesses to act in, partly as entertainment and diversion for them and the staff, and partly as a fundraiser for the Queen's war efforts. Crawfie also decided to continue the Girl Guides on the estate at Windsor, but this time with local girls (traveling was difficult and dangerous, they couldn't bring in their own crowd of young nobility). This was maybe the first time that Lilibet mixed with the children from the village, it was probably a refreshing surprise—they didn't curtsy, and they even dared call her Lilibet.

Besides the barbed wire and other measures taken to protect the young princesses, the Grenadier Guards were placed at Windsor for protection. Lilibet acted as hostess to these soldiers, getting to know them and including them in their activities. At age 16, young Elizabeth was named an honorary colonel in the Grenadier Guards. This protection did not immune her to the grief and suffering of war, though. Just as in other places the country, hot water was rationed at Windsor, the windows were blown out, and she got to know some of the guards protecting her who later fought and died overseas. Her mother wrote, "Lilibet meets young Grenadiers at Windsor, and then they get killed. It is horrid for someone so young." The young Elizabeth, sadly, got very good at sending letters to the guards' families, offering her heartfelt condolences and sympathies.

The young princesses became even more acquainted with grief when they lost a member of their own family. Their uncle, Prince George, Duke of Kent, the King's younger brother, was serving with the Royal Air Force during the war. In 1942 his plane crashed in Scotland on the way home from a mission. He was the first member of the royal family to die in battle in 500 years. The Windsors were mourning along with the rest of the country.

Lilibet was also worried about her parents in London. London during the Blitz was facing nightly bombing raids by the Luftwaffe; the destruction was awful and terrifying. Still, today if you walk down Exhibition Road you can see the chunks taken out of the side of the Victoria and Albert Museum, left as a reminder of Londoners' tenacity, suffering, and eventual victory. Buckingham Palace was hit by Luftwaffe bombs nine times during the war. The second bomb destroyed the chapel in the Palace and nearly killed the King and Queen. The King and Queen were sympathetic to the plight of their citizens; they wanted to stay with them and give them hope and reassurance. They went out among war-ravaged London and beyond, visiting hospitals,

evacuated children, and troops, raising money for the wool fund and metal drives, the Queen was just as visible as the King. Their efforts did not go unnoticed; they were hugely popular during the war, people saw them as brave and steadfast, serving their country in deeds just as they'd done in word.

With everything young Elizabeth was seeing and experiencing during the war, Lilibet wanted to do more to serve. Initially, her parents said it was just too dangerous for her, but they finally relented, and at age 18, in 1945, Elizabeth joined the Women's Auxiliary Territorial Service, the women's branch of the Army. She trained at the Mechanical Transport Training Centre with eleven other young women, most of whom were a few years older than she was, first learning to drive, then learning to change spark plugs, repair an engine, change a wheel, and drive a large army truck through heavy London traffic. She wore an olive drab uniform like everyone else and was called Second Subaltern Elizabeth Alexandra Mary Windsor. She said of the experience, "I've never worked so hard in my life. Everything I learnt was brand new to me." After a promotion five months later, she finished her service in the ATS as a junior commander. While she was never required to get a driver's license (she still doesn't have one, who would you even get to give the Queen her driving test?), this automotive experience started a lifelong love of driving and taught her skills that she is still proud of. Her short time in the ATS was the only time she felt like she could compare herself to other citizens and see how she stacked up, to interact freely with women her age. We have to imagine that she must have tried very hard to prove herself not just as a member of the royal family but as a member of the British public serving during wartime.

Young Elizabeth had few official royal duties until the war was nearing its end. In 1944, she was made Counsellor of State, a position which gave her power to act as a delegate for her father when he was unavailable, either because he was out of the country or, as often during wartime, was kept from traveling to where events were happening. It was during this time, and at just age 18, that Elizabeth signed a reprieve for a death sentence, causing her to wonder what brought the prisoner to such a state and what circumstances he must find himself in. It is a very empathetic and thoughtful response for someone so young and makes us think that she

had grown, learned, and seen quite a lot during the war years. That same year she also visited miners in Wales with her parents, launched her own battleship, gave public speeches, and attended her first official dinner at Buckingham Palace.

Finally, the war was over. Victory in Europe was celebrated on 8 May 1945, and Elizabeth and Margaret were as excited as the rest of the country. That evening she made a public appearance on the balcony at Buckingham Palace with her family to the cheers and tears of the crowds outside, then she and Margaret and a small crew of chaperones, among them Crawfie and Toni the French tutor as well as a few of the King's men, slipped out into the crowds. In her uniform so she wouldn't be recognized, she rode the buses, celebrated in the streets, and drank in the pubs, returning back to the palace in time to cheer on her parents again, but this time with the rest of the throng outside the palace gates. She and Margaret did the same thing the next night, enjoying the freedom of anonymity and justly feeling like she earned the celebrations along with the rest of the public, only sneaking back into the palace at 3:00 in the morning to make her companions sandwiches in the kitchens of the palace.

King George VI became a very prominent and visible supporter of his citizens and his wartime Prime Minister Winston Churchill, visiting troops on the front lines and making public speeches urging the British people to stay calm and carry on. Most of us are familiar with his 1939 address to the nation as the war starts (if nothing else, from The King's Speech, and if not, go watch it immediately, you won't be sorry). In this moving speech, he acknowledges that for most of his people this is the second war they will go through and that there will be dark days ahead but that they must stand firm and stand together. Yet even while he maintained a comforting presence for his people, he had a careful plan in place to remove Elizabeth and Margaret from Windsor or Buckingham Palace should the Germans invade London, with armored cars and dedicated guards at the ready. Thankfully, that was never necessary. Elizabeth saw her parents' bravery and service and the adoration the people had for them. Their dedication became a great lesson for her as she became monarch a few years later. Her own war service also brought her the experiences she would need as head of the armed forces. Indeed, she is the only female member of the royal family to have served in the armed forces, and the only living head of state who served in World War II—she could not have realized at the time what a meaningful and impressive accomplishment that would be throughout her many years of leadership.

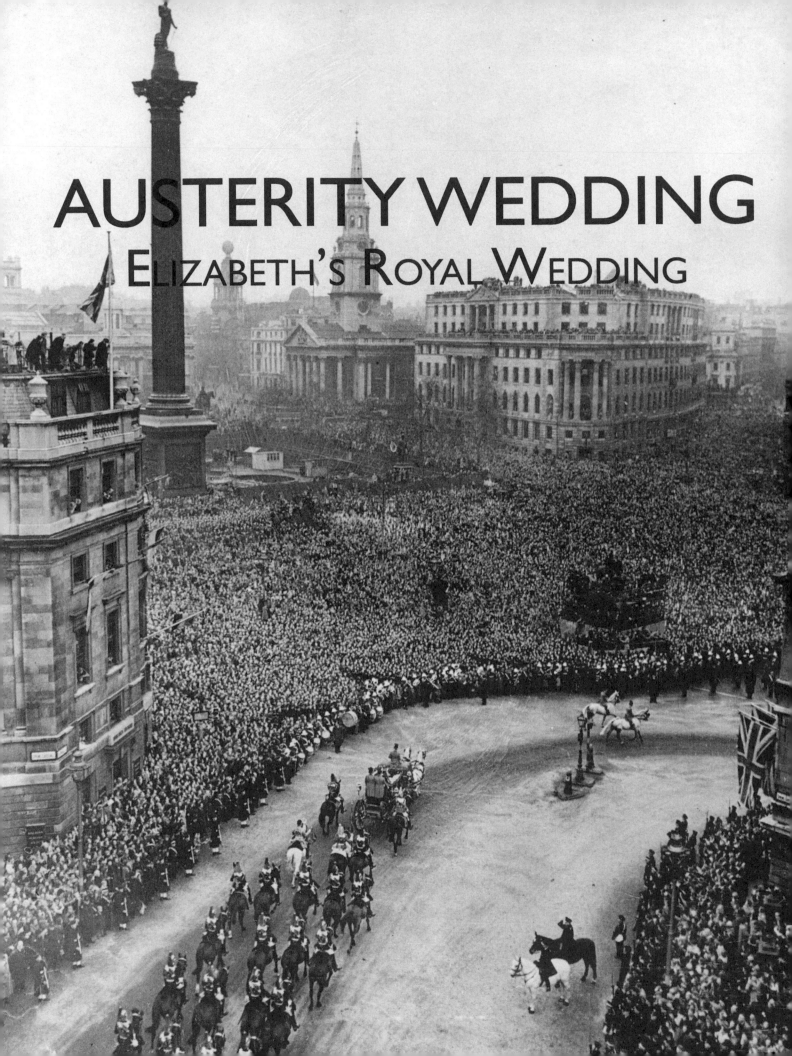

AUSTERITY WEDDING
Elizabeth's Royal Wedding

Most of us will remember the excitement surrounding Prince William and Catherine Middleton's wedding in 2011, and a lot of us will remember watching Charles and Diana's fairy tale wedding on TV when we were kids. Compared to those lavish affairs, Elizabeth and Philip's wedding was fairly restrained. It was, after all, only a few years since the end of the war and the country was still feeling the effects. England had been hit hard and was still suffering from empty farmland, empty factories, high unemployment and taxes, rationing, and a weakened economy. King George VI's Chancellor of the Exchequer called 1947, the year of Elizabeth's marriage, "annus horrendus," the horrendous year (and you know it must be bad if you have to express it in Latin). And yet, for Philip and Elizabeth, life looked grand.

Philip and Elizabeth were, like most royalty in Europe, related, sharing great-great-grandparents Queen Victoria and Prince Albert. As royal cousins, they came across each other several times in their younger years, at family weddings and at the coronation of Elizabeth's father. But it wasn't until 1939 when Elizabeth was 13 and Philip was 18 that the relationship really started to take hold. Philip was a young, handsome, dashing cadet at the Royal Naval College in Dartmouth when Elizabeth went for a visit with her parents and Margaret. Elizabeth was smitten from the start, Philip maybe not so much (she was, after all, 13, and this wasn't Romeo and Juliet). Ever the social climber, Philip's uncle and Elizabeth's cousin, Lord Louis Mountbatten, affectionately known as Uncle Dickie, arranged for Philip to be invited to tea at the palace shortly after. Crawfie, the princesses' nanny, noticed that Elizabeth "never took her eyes off him," even though Philip didn't seem to notice. Soon it was the war years, yet Philip made several visits to see the family at Windsor, and Elizabeth wrote to him while he was serving with the Royal Navy in the Mediterranean and the Pacific. As we remember from our last article, Elizabeth did a lot of growing up during the war years, and by the time Philip returned, he was paying her quite a lot of attention. As their cousin, Patricia Mountbatten recalls, "she would not have been a difficult person to love," and Crawfie described him saying, "He came into the Palace like a refreshing sea breeze."

But what was Philip's story and could he have possibly been worthy of marrying the future Queen of England, so beloved by her parents? Elizabeth's mother and quite a few others didn't think so, at least not at first. Philip was born Prince Philip of Greece and Denmark in Corfu just before a coup when his family was exiled from Greece. He was raised in Paris in an unhappy and unloving home. His father spent a lot of time with his girlfriends, and his mother soon had a nervous breakdown and left to join a convent. He was fond of his sisters, but most of them married Nazis or suspected Nazi-sympathizers, and one of them, Cecilia, and her family died in a plane crash while Philip was at school in Scotland. Philip was very much on his own. At the age of 8, Philip was sent off to boarding school and from then on was, in essence, homeless and neglected by his family. He first went to school in Germany, but only for a year when the war forced him to move on to Gordonstoun School in Scotland (the school in that horrible episode of The Crown, you may remember). While the school may have been difficult, Philip was fairly happy there, learning leadership, service, and hard work. He was even made Head Boy (and without older brothers there, we can assume he wasn't teased the same was Percy Weasley was in Harry Potter when he was named "Bighead Boy.") Uncle Dickie took a lot of interest in young Philip, nurturing his education and leadership skills, and Philip grew up well—handsome, athletic, intelligent, clever.

Philip, however, had neither money nor land and was not considered English enough to marry Elizabeth. And yet, Elizabeth's family—the Windsors—only became "Windsors" during World War I when their Germanic background and last name became problematic. George V, in 1917, changed the family name from Saxe-Coburg-Gotha (Prince Albert was German, and Victoria took his name at their wedding) to Windsor; George III was the first Hanoverian born in England, his father and grandfather, Kings George I and II didn't even speak English. Philip's mother was a British citizen and was born at Windsor Castle; Philip was educated in Britain and didn't even remember living in Greece and was by this time a decorated sailor in the British Royal Navy; he had also already dropped his Germanic family name and had taken his mother's British name of Mountbatten; he converted to Church of England. Calling him not British enough seemed a little "pot calling the kettle black." The

Elizabeth was so young, just 20 years old when Philip proposed on a family trip to Balmoral in 1946. Philip had been to Balmoral before, in 1944, when he spent a very pleasant, happy vacation with the royal family. It was a trip that would have stood out in contrast to his unhappy, dysfunctional family life. The Windsors loved to play together—games, hunting, tag—something Philip didn't do with his own family. The Windsors liked each other.

King George was impressed with Philip's naval record, his intelligence, and his effect on Lilibet, and Elizabeth's mother was coming around. After that trip to Balmoral, Philip was often seen driving his little black MG roadster up to the private entrance at Buckingham Palace, wandering around the palace in his shirtsleeves, and treating Elizabeth

just like he would have treated any other girl, a refreshing and surprising turn of events for the royal family. While he could be testy, hot-tempered, and impulsive, he was also attentive and witty and seemed to be comfortable enough with the royal family. By the time Philip went to Balmoral again two years later, Elizabeth accepted his proposal immediately, without consulting her parents (although we can imagine that the topic had come up with them before), and Philip commented that he was pleasantly surprised "to have fallen in love completely and unreservedly."

The family chose not to announce the engagement publicly for a while, instead of taking one last royal family tour together as just "we four." The King and Queen and their daughters spent three months in Africa plus another month traveling round trip by boat. While they were separated, Elizabeth and Philip wrote to each other faithfully, and while she was away, Philip was busy preparing. With the help of Uncle Dickie, Lord Mountbatten, Philip renounced his titles as Prince of Greece and Denmark and became a British Citizen, which turned out to be unnecessary considering his mother was born at Windsor. And as a wedding present, he gave up smoking. On the family's return, and after a royal engagement party at Buckingham Palace, just before the wedding, the King named Philip Duke of Edinburgh, the title by which he's called today, as well as Earl of Merioneth and Baron Greenwich, although not Prince Consort as Prince Albert had been named. It was also decreed that Philip would be called His Royal Highness, and he was given the Order of the Garter, the highest honor the King can confer. Giving up his title as Prince of Greece and Denmark didn't seem to do Philip any harm.

The wedding took place on 20 November 1947. Elizabeth used her wartime rations, still in place, to buy the fabric for her wedding dress, the royal family was conscious of appearing too extravagant during the country's difficulties. And still, the country and the Commonwealth were eager to celebrate with the family. They received thousands of letters and telegrams wishing them well, Gandhi sent a loincloth (the family found this funny and had to assume it was unused). The crowds turned out in the tens of thousands in the cold to watch the procession of the King and Princess Elizabeth in the Irish State Coach on the way to Westminster Abbey. Winston Churchill called the whole affair "a flash of color on the hard road we have to travel."

Inside the church were some two thousand guests, among them heads of state from around the world, Philip's mother and sisters (not their husbands, and his father was already dead by this point), and no former King Edward now just Duke of Windsor. He was no longer invited to family events. Reports tell of Elizabeth looking calm and lovely with Philip by his side in his dress uniform.

For the procession out of the Abbey, Elizabeth switched to the Glass Coach, this time with Philip by her side. They were accompanied by the Household Cavalry and 100,000 people cheering in the streets. They returned to a relatively small luncheon (trying again to be respectful of post-war austerity) of 150 people at Buckingham Palace, where Philip cut the wedding cake with his sword.

After all the wedding festivities, the couple was off on their honeymoon, leaving from Waterloo Station with Elizabeth's dog and a small crew of private staff. They spent their first week in Hampshire and another two weeks on the grounds at Balmoral. In a letter to her parents, Elizabeth wrote, "Philip is an angel—he is so kind and thoughtful." And Philip also wrote to Elizabeth's mother, saying that Elizabeth is "the only thing in this world which is absolutely real to me, and my ambition is to weld the two of us into a newly combined existence that will not only be able to withstand the shocks directed at us but will also have a positive existence for the good." Philip already seemed to be aware that this would, at times, be a difficult relationship to navigate. Upon returning to London, he was able to keep working, for a time, with the Navy, which is what he was hoping for. The couple lived next to St. James's Palace at Clarence House, and Philip could walk to the Admiralty every day for work. Elizabeth worked at home and at Buckingham Palace with her private secretary, Jock Colville, learning how the government and the monarchy operated. This was a good time for the couple.

Philip and Elizabeth seemed to be well suited for each other, adoring of each other and complementary in their skills and personalities. They were both crazy drivers—Elizabeth in the years to come would have at least two formal complaints filed against her reckless driving, and Philip would later crash his car just after giving a speech on road safety. Crashing his car seemed to be a not uncommon occurrence for him, common enough that the chauffeurs at the Palace were reluctant to let him drive their cars. Philip's dry wit and complete willingness to say whatever was on his mind helped lighten many situations, with him commenting to his cousin Patricia's husband, when he noticed how lovely Elizabeth's skin was, "yes, she's like that all over." Elizabeth's secretary, Martin Charteris, said later, "Prince Philip is the only man in the world who treats the Queen simply as another human being." We have to assume their life was never dull. Their treatment of and fondness for each appeared to be just what Elizabeth and Philip needed; they were off to a good start together.

NOTES FROM A ROYAL WEDDING

By Jonathan Thomas

It was one perfect moment. It was a moment that it seemed like the whole world was watching. The doors opened, the trumpets sounded, and there was a woman, entering a church to marry the man she loved. It felt as if almost the whole world had stopped in silence to watch. I'm an approaching middle-aged Straight White American Man, and it brought me to tears. Who doesn't love weddings? But Royal Weddings? Those are something extra special. And I was there to see it all.

What really struck me was the silence. Granted, there was plenty going on in the church. I'm talking about the silence in Windsor. Minutes ago, there were cheering crowds. And then, silence. You could hear a pin drop in Windsor. Windsor paused. The world paused. Two lovers got married. And we all rejoiced.

Windsor was really the perfect place for a Royal Wedding. When it was announced that the wedding and festivities would take place in Windsor. I was dubious.

Surely not in tiny Windsor?

There was no way they could handle the crowds.

They could, and they did.

The British know how to prepare for events like this, and they did it with aplomb. Windsor did the job beautifully. They managed the crowds perfectly. The down was resplendent in Union Jacks and patriotic decorations. And not just the 'official' decorations. Many private homes when out of their way to show their excitement for the day. As an American Anglophile, I was chuffed to bits to see the American flag just as much as the Union Jack. Brits really embraced Meghan's American-ness. It was truly lovely to see.

On the big day itself, there was a veritable panoply of characters out on the streets of Windsor. There were plenty of Americans, waving the stars & stripes from the behind the barriers. There were Brits in costume - from town criers to pretend soldiers. And then there were the Brits who looked like they were in costume, but actually, they were dressed normally (insert image of the country gentleman in a tweed cap. Some women were even in formal dress - I even saw a wedding dress or two. And then there were the hats - the glorious hats. If you can't wear a fabulous hat at a Royal Wedding, then what's the point?

But by far the best 'cosplayer' I saw in the crowds was the chap who was dressed as Mr. Bean. Tweed jacket, teddy bear, suitcase and all. I had to do a double take to make sure he wasn't actually Rowan Atkinson in character. He was a popular chap to get a picture with, and he seemed to be eating up the attention. And honestly, and this is rather uncharitable of me, if you look like Mr. Bean, you have to take the positive attention when you can get it!

For many people in Windsor that day, it was a day of work. Everyone had a bit part play to make the day great. Of course, there were the police keeping everyone safe. And I'm always amazed at events like this - the police are never intimidating, even when you see armed ones. There was medical personnel throughout the crowds in case anyone needed attention quickly. The street cleaners entertained crowds keeping the streets clean. Then there were the grafters.

And who were they? Well, no event like this would be complete without street sellers hawking flags, scarves, face masks and a kaleidoscope of other Royal Wedding-related tat. I don't use that word to criticise. These people play a critical role, and I bought a flag myself from them. They work their arses off on days like this, and they deserve any penny they earn. It's the hardest work you can do during an event like this. We can't forget the small army of food vendors who camped out along The Long Walk, offering the most critical ingredients to a Grand Royal Day Out: endless cups of tea and endless cones of chips (that's fries to you and me).

During the last Royal Wedding, I was really intrigued to see such a wide range of people who had come out to watch the wedding. I was pleased to see much of the same for Harry & Meghan's wedding. I was really surprised at how many Americans there were in the crowds. Typically when I'm in England, hearing an American accent (at least outside of London) causes me to pause and feel a pang of patriotism. I would say there were tens of thousands of Americans who made the journey to Windsor to watch their fellow countrywoman wed into the British Royal family.

Looking at the crowds, it was a wide range of peoples and races. It was really a testament to Britain's diversity, and the legacy of its Empire and now Commonwealth that so many different types of people were represented in the crowds.

The British get a bad rap as being a people of closet racists and xenophobes, and while every culture has a subsection of close-minded people, the British are an open and welcoming people. If you don't believe me, just look at the pictures of the crowds from the day. Britain is diverse, and in its current struggles, it will take great strength from that. The wedding itself was a massive symbol of how much 'conservative' Britain has changed in the last 30 or so years. In the days of Princess Diana, it would have been unthinkable for a member of the British Royal Family to marry an American, let alone someone of a different race (and previously divorced and not Anglican!). The fact the event happened at all is a testament to how much Britain has changed for the better. And most people just didn't bloody care, and that's the way it should be (and the ones who did care and shared their racist views, were easily drowned out by how positive everyone was about it).

My experience at this wedding was much different than when I came to see Will & Kate get married back in 2011. Then, I got up before dawn and made my way to The Mall to get a spot right outside Buckingham Palace, then proceeded to stand there for a good 6 hours. It was brutal on my legs and my bladder. It was also a very hot day. And then when the crowds descended on the palace for the Wave and Flypast, it became a crush of hundreds of thousands people. It was both exhilarating and downright scary. I was so worried Windsor would turn into that, and I'm so glad it just didn't.

Instead of being on the streets, waiting with everyone for all the events to unfold, I spent the morning and afternoon in the ballroom at the Castle Hotel, hosted by the Foreign Press Association. This HQ for the foreign press provided fast WiFi, TV screens to watch, tea & biscuits and everything else reported would need to cover such a big occasion. Before I left for the trip, I was quite worried that being sequestered in the room all day would ruin the experience for me. I wouldn't be down on the streets with everyone else.

But, honestly, it didn't. I had a bloody great day. While I wanted to enjoy the day as a spectator, I was there to work. And the facilities provided by the FPA allowed me to work without interruption and do everything we planned to do on the day.

The Castle Hotel was central enough, it's literally right across the street from Windsor Castle, that you still very much felt a part of events going on outside. You could hear the crowd cheer. You could hear their silence.

And when the big moment came, and it was time for the carriage procession to go by the hotel, I was able to pop outside, set up my cameras and actually get pictures and videos of the happy royal couple as they rode past. I didn't have to wake up ridiculously early, and I didn't have to deal with a massive crowd. It was the best of both worlds. I got to be there and experience the essential bits, and I was able to do it on my own terms.

It's hard to describe that feeling when they ride by. I felt it just the same when Will & Kate rode by me during their wedding. It's a massive thrill. The crowd is loud and cheering with anticipation. But then the crowd gets louder, but not all at once. They get louder in a wave. As the carriage passes people, the wave of sound follows them. The roar gets louder and louder as they approach to the point it's almost deafening. Then they clip-clop their way by and the roar recedes as they ride away. It's a huge feeling of excitement. Of shared experience. You've all just seen something wonderful.

And then it's all over.

Our world can be a terrible place. It's easy to get lost in all the bad political news and latest stories of violence all over the world and be depressed about it. Whether you hate the political situation in your country or elsewhere, a Royal Wedding is above all that. It's simply a happy event. Two beautiful young people are professing their love for each other for the whole world to see. And for one moment, we all stop to watch. For one moment, the world isn't such a terrible place. This is what it means to be human, to find small pockets of joy in life, even amongst absolute misery.

I felt only one thing as they rode by me on the carriage procession: absolute contentment. If I had my own state of nirvana, that would be it. In my mind, all was right with the world. But it's only a moment, and it's fleeting. I had to run back to the hotel to process my images and video. Once the headlines of the wedding recede, the bad news of the world slowly creeps back in, and the world returns to normal. Hoping that it can have another moment to pause and look out in wonder.

Once the festivities were over and I returned to the streets of Windsor, it was now late in the afternoon. The scene was massively changed. The crowds were gone from the main streets in Windsor. The campers had gone. Everyone with their silly hats had made their way back to Windsor's train stations to begin their long journeys home. Wedding-related ephemera littered the streets, blowing in the wind as cleaning crews started the long process of cleaning it all up.

Walking into the side streets, the day had turned into just another Saturday in Windsor, England. The sun was shining, casting a late afternoon golden glow on Windsor's Medieval and Georgian buildings. The weather was warm, and the sky was clear of clouds. People were out shopping on the high street. Eating food in the restaurants. Arguing with spouses. Arguing with children. A few hours about it was Britain at its finest, on show for the world. Now, it was Britain as it always is, which to me, is a much more interesting show. Airplanes, abnormally diverted away from Windsor during the wedding, returned to the flights above the city.

When I came back into Windsor the next day, a Sunday, to catch the train to Oxford, it was a completely changed place. If you weren't aware already, it was not clear that there was a Royal Wedding the previous day. All the street barriers were gone. The mess was cleaned up. The only crowds present were the regular tourists on a day trip to Windsor. It was all rather surreal.

It showed how fleeting this one event was. As someone who is part of the generation that grew up with William and Harry, watching both of them get married was a seminal event, not just in my life but in British history. Harry's wedding was the last royal wedding for at least 20-30 years (and I mean in the immediate direct line of succession, there will be smaller Royal Do's, but they won't have this kind of importance). By the time there is another Royal Wedding, I will be in my 50s or 60s, and my own children will be getting married (hopefully). It was genuinely fulfilling and special to be a part of two major events, even in my own small way. There will be other major Royal Events in the coming years (and I hate to say it, a Coronation, long away may that be), but for weddings, this was it.

And what a way to go out. As I sat in my flat, exhausted from a long day, and watched the Royal Couple drive away in their electric Jaguar to their party at Frogmore House into the sunset, I thought how lovely it had all been and to have been there.

May their marriage be long and happy.

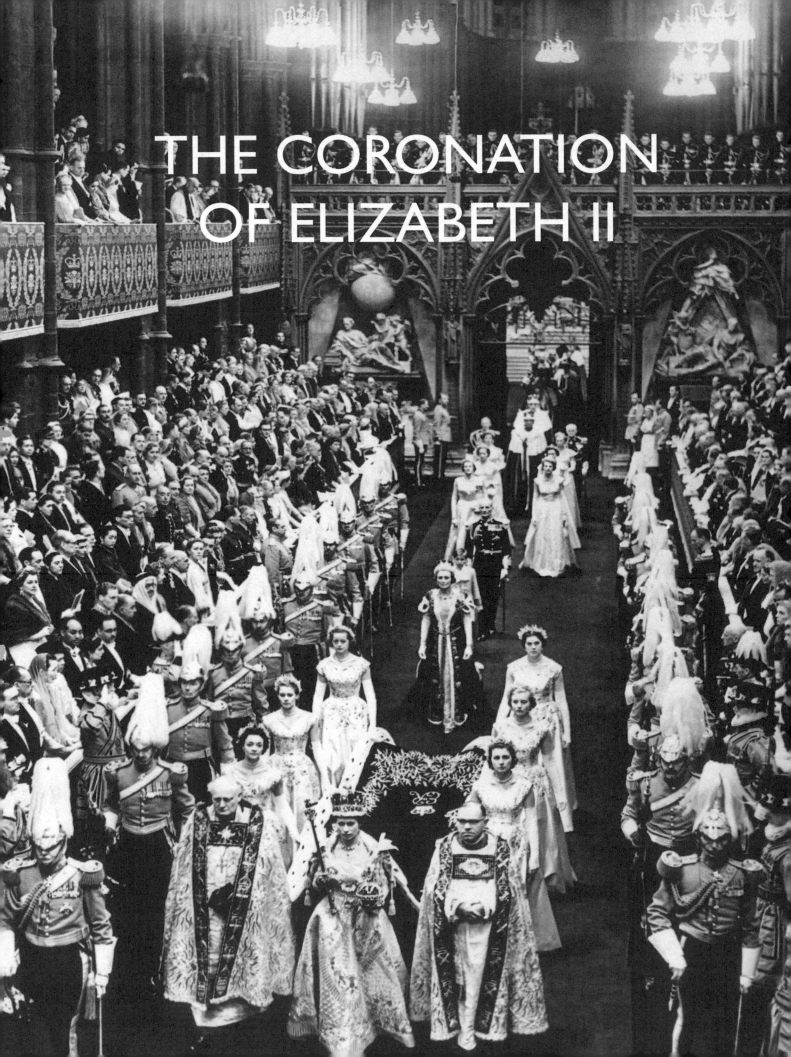

THE CORONATION OF ELIZABETH II

When Princess Elizabeth and Margaret's father was unexpectedly crowned George VI in 1936, after King Edward VIII's abdication, Margaret asked if her sister would now have to be Queen. "Yes, someday," Lilibet responded. "Poor you," Margaret said. Elizabeth's Coronation would take place a whole lot sooner than any of them could have expected, with King George's early death from lung cancer at age 56, just 16 years later when Elizabeth was only 25 years old.

Elizabeth's father's health began to fail as early as 1948, and soon, the King was very ill. Elizabeth was taking on more royal responsibilities and was being prepared for them. In 1947 she was assigned her own private secretary, Jock Colville, who had also been a secretary to Neville Chamberlain and Winston Churchill during World War II. He was very knowledgeable and the perfect one to school Elizabeth in not just royal duties but the workings of the government and her place in it. He also arranged for her to travel as a way for her to learn more about the country and Commonwealth.

By 1951 the King's absence from public life became widely known, when King George VI was too unwell to attend the Trooping of the Colour and Elizabeth had to attend and ride in his stead. The Trooping of the Colour is the annual celebration of the monarch's birthday, celebrated in June (no matter when the monarch's birthday actually is, the same way Americans observe Washington's or Lincoln's birthday on a convenient Monday instead of their actual birthdays) at Horse Guards Parade, with about 1000 guards and cavalry on parade and the monarch riding alongside. It's a huge event and something the King would not usually miss, making his absence remarkable and conspicuous.

This same year also marked, in essence, the end of Prince Philip's naval career. He had been stationed in Malta, yet was called home to attend to more and more royal duties with Elizabeth. At just age 30, Philip was sorry to see the end of his naval career, yet rather accepting of the path ahead: "I thought I was going to have a career in the Navy, but it became obvious there was no hope . . . There was no choice. It just happened. You have to make compromises. That's life. I accepted it. I tried to make the best of it." For all of Philip's grumpiness about royal life, we can appreciate his honesty and stoic attitude towards his family and his duty. It's an attitude he has repeated often and has served him well throughout his years in the royal family.

Elizabeth and Philip had postponed a Commonwealth tour because of the King's ailing health, but in January 1952 decided to go ahead on a six-month tour of Australia, New Zealand, and the Pacific, with a stop in Kenya first. It was in Kenya while staying at Treetops Hotel, with Elizabeth enjoying her new-found hobby of photography, that the King died. On February 6th, Martin Charteris, Elizabeth's secretary who was staying at a different hotel than Elizabeth and Philip, called Philip's secretary to tell him that the King had died in his sleep. Charteris had a plan ready for this eventuality, traveling with accession papers and mourning clothes for Elizabeth, and kindly deciding that Philip was the best one to tell Elizabeth about her father's death.

Even at such a young age, Elizabeth took the news well, sad but not emotional, expressing regret to her staff and the Commonwealth that their tour would now be cut short. Her mother told Queen Mary, her grandmother, "I cannot bear to think of Lilibet so young to bear such a burden." She would begin ruling immediately, even though her Coronation would not take place for another 16 months, taking the throne at the same age as the first Queen Elizabeth, as the 40th monarch of England since William the Conqueror took the throne in 1066.

To bring her new place as sovereign into sharp focus, meeting her plane returning from Kenya was Winston Churchill, her first prime minister and by now an old friend. The next day she traveled to St. James's Palace, formerly the London home of the monarchs and the ceremonial home of the Accession Council. It was here that she took her oath in front of the senior advisers, politicians, and clergy as well as Prince Philip--her first royal duty as the new sovereign. She told the Accession Council, "My heart is too full for me to say more to you today than I shall always work, as my father did throughout his reign, to advance the happiness and prosperity of my peoples, spread as they are the world over. . . . I pray that God will help me to discharge worthily this heavy task that has been lain upon me so early in my life."

The press called it a New Elizabethan Age, and a young politician by the name of Margaret

Thatcher commented, "if, as many earnestly pray, the accession of Elizabeth II can help to remove the last shreds of prejudice against women aspiring to the highest places, then a new era for women will indeed be at hand." The new Queen Elizabeth stepped into her role immediately, even calmly, "Extraordinary thing, I no longer feel anxious or worried. I don't know what it is--but I have lost all my timidity." About a month later, Elizabeth and Philip and their two young children, Charles and Anne, moved into Buckingham Palace, just down the street from where they had been living, and Elizabeth began what would be her daily routine for the rest of her reign. Rising at 7:30 every morning, having breakfast, being serenaded by a bagpiper under her window at 9:00 every morning, just as Victoria had done during her reign, a quick visit with her children, then off to official business and her red boxes containing her daily government papers to review. These red boxes would become a fixture for the Queen; even on vacation she rarely missed a day, and it was these official daily briefings that kept her abreast of everything she would need to know, causing her long list of Prime Ministers and advisers to comment on how intelligent she was and how nothing got past her— she was constantly surprising people with her

knowledge of the daily happenings in politics and the Commonwealth.

The Queen Mother, choosing not to be called the Dowager Queen now that she was widowed, took on a new role as well. Winston Churchill urged her not to go into hiding with decades of mourning as Queen Victoria had on the death of Prince Albert, advice that the Queen Mother took to heart, becoming the national grandmother, living by her motto "The point of human life and living is to give and to create new goodness all the time." She was a constant presence in the palace and royal life, maintaining her closeness with her daughter the Queen, knowing that they were really the only two people alive who knew what it was like to be them. On their daily phone calls, the palace operator would connect the Queen Mother with Queen Elizabeth, saying, "Good morning, Your Majesty, Her Majesty is on the line for Your Majesty." Elizabeth's grandmother, Queen Mary, would die in 1953 before the Coronation, the two Queen Elizabeths were in a tiny club.

The new Queen was incredibly popular, gaining steam in the lead-up to the Coronation on June 2nd 1953. In her first Christmas broadcast, still in 1952, she spoke warmly and humbly, "I want to ask you all, whatever your religion may be, to pray for me on that day--to pray that God may give me wisdom and strength to carry out the solemn promises I shall be making and that I may faithfully serve Him and you, all the days of my life." In the year or so leading up to the Coronation, Philip took over the task of planning the big event, a good job for someone who was now without a job and was a great manager and innovator. Philip loved new technology, and the biggest new technology at this time was television. Philip wanted to televise the Coronation, Elizabeth and the Archbishop of Canterbury disagreed, thinking it would cheapen the event. But the people wanted the event televised, and Elizabeth soon gave in, well, mostly. The anointing, the most sacred part of the ceremony, would remain un-televised, taking place under a canopy; there would also be no close-ups, just a bird' s-eye view of the ceremony. As far as Elizabeth, also the Head of the Church of England, was concerned, the anointing sanctified her before God to serve her people. One of the Archbishop's senior chaplains put it this way: "The real significance of the Coronation for her was the anointing, not the crowning. She was consecrated, and that makes her Queen. It is the most solemn thing that has ever happened in her life. She cannot abdicate. She is there until death."

Televising the ceremony turned out to be a great idea--sales of TVs in Britain spiked in the week before the Coronation, doubling the number of people owning a TV, no small feat for a country still recovering from World War II. Of the 36 million people in Britain in 1953, 27 million of them watched the ceremony on TV, including a young John Major, her future Prime Minister, and a young Paul McCartney who later said, "It was a thrilling time. I grew up with the Queen, thinking she was a babe. She was beautiful and glamorous." A third of Americans watched from home, as well.

Elizabeth took her Coronation very seriously, practicing in the weeks leading up to the event. The robes alone weighed 36 pounds, she wore those around the palace along with St. Edward's Crown, practicing walking so she could do it without wobbling. The Archbishop tried to practice, as well, in rehearsals at Westminster Abbey, although his help might have been less helpful, tripping down the stairs as he was showing the Queen's maids of honor how to walk up the stairs successfully. To those voicing their concern about Elizabeth's

stamina for the three-hour-long ceremony dating back to the first Coronation in the Abbey in 1066, she easily replied, "I'll be alright. I'm as strong as a horse." And she was, the Coronation came off without a hitch, causing her to remark upon returning to the palace when it was all over, "Oh that was marvelous. Nothing went wrong!"

The crowds loved it, as well, even in the rain. The processional route from Buckingham Palace to Westminster Abbey was lined the night before with tens of thousands of people waiting to catch a glimpse of the young Queen. Philip and Elizabeth were mindful of the post-war austerity and didn't want to overdo the event, but there were still twenty-nine bands and twenty-seven carriages full of dignitaries from around the world, along with 13,000 soldiers from around the Commonwealth in the parade. People were ready to celebrate, and Prince Philip looked dashing in his full dress uniform with the Queen wearing Queen Victoria's diadem (which we know from Harry Potter is a kind of tiara, this one rather stunning and bejeweled). Uncle David, Duke of Windsor and the brief King Edward VIII, was not invited, Churchill saying it would have been "quite inappropriate for a King who had abdicated."

After the ceremony, canons were fired at Hyde Park and the Tower of London to celebrate, followed by another processional back to Buckingham Palace, with Elizabeth now in the more comfortable Imperial State Crown, where the Queen and Prince Philip entertained a relatively small crowd of mostly royal family and friends. It was at this luncheon that the newest recipe was served—Coronation Chicken, a cold chicken and mayonnaise salad now found in every Pret-a-Manger in Britain. After what we can only imagine was an incredibly long day for Queen Elizabeth, now with the official title "Her Majesty Elizabeth the Second, by the Grace of God, of the United Kingdom of Great Britain and Northern Ireland, and of Her Other Realms and Territories Queen, Head of the Commonwealth, Defender of the Faith," she still had the energy for a short radio broadcast that evening, telling her people, "Throughout all my life and with all my heart I shall strive to be worthy of your trust." The twenty-five-year-old Queen and mother of two was well on her way.

WHAT THE QUEEN MEANS TO ME

By Jonathan Thomas

I saw the Queen once. This is not a hard thing for a British person to do. Well, maybe now that she's older. But when she was in her public events prime, you could count on seeing the Queen a few times in your life. I'm not British and for me, seeing the Queen was a once in a lifetime event. I'm happy to report I have actually seen her with my own two eyes.

I was standing on the Mall, the stately road that leads from Buckingham Palace to Whitehall and beyond during the royal wedding of Prince William and Kate Middleton. I'd woken up at 5:00 a.m. to get my spot on the Mall. I was lucky I'd had an interview with BBC Radio that morning; I was already within the media scrum area, so when I exited, all I had to do was sidle my way to a spot on the Mall. I was in the perfect spot to see everything happen.

It was a very long, boring morning until things started happening. Every slight movement that might have been interesting elicited excitement in the crowds. Even the street sweepers made the crowds cheer. Finally, the procession of fancy Rolls-Royces and Mercedes began as they all made their way to Westminster Abbey. I was close enough that I could clearly see the gates into the Buckingham Palace forecourt. As the ceremonies began and the loudspeakers boomed with preparations, the gates opened and a scarlet Rolls-Royce pulled out. The first thing I saw was the hat.

Then, I saw her.

Her Majesty in all her understated glory. HM, The Queen. I could see her smiling. I even took a picture. I almost teared up.

It's really strange, being an American and loving the head of state of another nation. But I do. Let's face it; elected presidents are nothing compared to a monarch. When we got rid of the British king, we decided to set up a system that was somewhat similar but instead of a king, we elected a president. As the years went on, despite the desire to not have a king, the presidency turned into a pseudo-monarchy. Our presidents don't inspire affection like a monarch does.

The Queen represents the entire nation of the United Kingdom (and her Commonwealth realms). Her government, which rules in her name, are the ones answerable to voters and they never have the same level of affection and popularity as the Queen has had - except maybe for Winston Churchill who basically had a king's funeral when he died. No, the Queen is Britain, and Britain is the Queen.

As I'm the same age as Prince William and a little older than Harry, my childhood mirrors their childhoods. Well, generationally, we literally could not have more in common than that! Princess Diana was a huge part of my childhood. My mother was an Anglophile, so she paid attention to all the Diana and Charles drama. Diana and the Royal Family just existed in the background of my life growing up. I saw the news stories about the marriage troubles, and I saw countless new stories about their kids. When I was very young, I would always watch CNN headline news right before school because I always loved to be informed about the day's news. The British Royal Family always seemed to be in the news.

It was a death that really began my fascination with the Royal Family.

When Diana died, I was just thirteen years old. I was in the phase of my life where my interest in Diana was merely, "She's hot," because I was getting quite tired of all the gossip at the time. But one night in August, I returned from an evening out at the local mall, when going to the mall was still a thing people did, and turned on the TV to see the news that Princess Diana had died in a car accident.

I was simultaneously devastated by the news and enthralled by it. It was the first real major royal event I remember witnessing via the media. I was glued to the TV for the next few weeks as all the details were revealed and pundits had endless debates about her death and what it meant for the Royal Family. The film The Queen starring Helen Mirren would later become one of my favorite films, but the interesting thing is that I had no idea what was really going on.

I just remember the Queen making a speech from Buckingham Palace and it being a really big deal. I just found it all really sad, and it made me sad.

I remember watching the funeral when it happened. It was broadcast on American TV. There was great interest here. I watched as Prince William and Harry walked behind the gun carriage that carried their mother's casket through central London. I was very sad for them. Prince William and I were close in age, and I couldn't imagine losing my mother and being practically alone to face that loss.

It was all a terrible tragedy, but from that tragedy came my great interest in the Royal Family and Britain itself as I became hungry to learn as much as I could about it all. I learned how Britain does great state events. I learned that the nation had changed from one proud of its stiff upper lip to one that was willing to mourn in public. I learned that maybe the Royal Family wasn't as great of an organization as I thought. My final memory of that terrible time was watching Diana's funeral hearse being followed through the green beautiful, rolling English countryside with golden sunlight overhead and roads lined with thousands of people just trying to pay their final respects.

Of course, now I know a lot more about what was really happening behind the scenes during that dark time. The Queen made a lot of mistakes. Despite what the Royal Family tries to get across, she is not a perfect, saintly woman. And that's okay. She's human. Still, she's a very good human. The best of us. She was never supposed to be Queen, but when it became clear she was going to be, she dedicated her life to being the best monarch she possibly could. The amount of affection she engenders in the average British person is astonishing.

I've never met a British person that hates the Queen or wants to get rid of the Royal Family. Oh, they'll take the piss out of them (they are quite weird). Prince Charles doesn't inspire nearly the same amount of affection as his mother does, and he never will. She represents the rock solid core of Britain and what it means to be British. She's permanence in an impermanent world. She's respect. She's deference. She's a symbol of an entire people. The monarch in Britain never technically dies. It literally contin-ues immediately to the next person. She's in her 90s now, and the fact that she's still performing public duties is simply astonishing.

Every time there's a major royal event, the TV networks roll out the usual suspects from the Republican movement. Those are the folks who think the monarchy should be abolished, that they are a waste of money, and their existence fosters a culture based on class inequality. They're not completely wrong. Though, the Royal Family brings far more into Britain than it costs them. It's quite a bargain, actually. But even when you hear these people being interviewed, it's very clear that their hearts are not completely into the Republican movement. Britain having an elected president or head of state is such an out there concept, I don't think it's something that would ever happen.

Many Royal commentators say, "Well, just wait until Charles is king."

Yeah, no. That's not the way monarchies work. Look, he'll never be as popular as his mother, but I think Charles will be a decent enough king. The British Royal Family is so well respected and held in such high esteem that sixteen independent nations still choose to have her as their head of state. That's so bizarre. You have a country like Canada, our neighbors to the north and they still love their Queen. And that's the thing, all the countries think of her as their Queen. She's not just the British Queen. Even in the country of Australia, where Republicanism is much stronger, they still failed to abolish the monarchy when it was put to a referendum.

One day I hope to become a British citizen and part of that process will be that I'll have to swear an oath to the Queen. I will do it with all my heart and all my loyalty even if it's Charles by that point. God save the Queen (or King)!

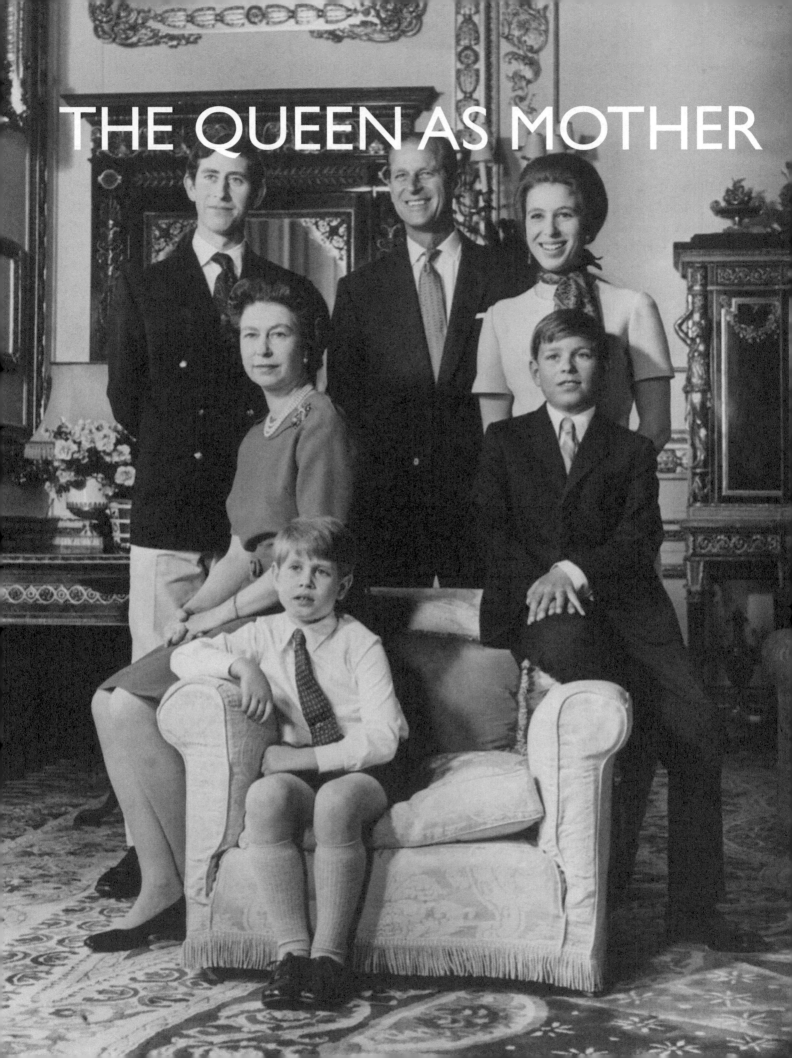

THE QUEEN AS MOTHER

People seem to have a lot of opinions about Queen Elizabeth II's mothering skills. For good or bad we see her four children, now grown, in the press quite a lot.

Elizabeth took the throne in 1952 upon the death of her father, King George VI, when her son Charles was not quite four, and Anne was not yet two, and before their births, she was already busy with royal duties as her father's health failed. We can see pictures from the Coronation of young Charles and Anne watching from the sidelines. As a woman and the monarch, the Queen is expected to be king and Queen and mother all at the same time. She took all those roles very seriously and worked hard to juggle her royal duties and motherhood, while saying in a letter to her parents from her honeymoon, "I only hope that I can bring up my children in the happy atmosphere of love and fairness which Margaret and I have grown up in."

The first thing Philip and Elizabeth had to decide was what the children would be called—their surname. Philip and his uncle and closest family member Dickie Mountbatten were excited to think the name Mountbatten would be the new name of the heirs to the throne. Elizabeth, however, took the advice of family, advisers, and Prime Minister Winston Churchill, and insisted on her children keeping her family's name—Windsor.

This would be a bone of contention in the family for years to come, Philip taking it particularly hard:

"I'm nothing but a bloody amoeba ... I am the only man in the country not allowed to give his name to his children." It was enough a topic of conversation that in 1960 Elizabeth decided that their direct descendants who were not called Prince or Princess (not heirs to the throne) would be named Mountbatten-Windsor. This seemed to be the concession she could make to Philip's family name.

Philip became the primary ruler of the children, kind of like the stay-at-home dad of today. He made most of the daily decisions for the children's activities and education, even scheduling time with each child individually on a regular basis. But Elizabeth was not un-involved. Once she was crowned Queen, one of the first things she did was change the time of her weekly meeting with the Prime Minister to Tuesday evenings at 6:30 so that she could do bathtime and bedtime with the children. She was also the first monarch to stop making her children bow and curtsy to the monarch--we have to think they would be grateful for that. And when she was in town, she spent time with her young children at 9:30 in the morning before spending the day on her work, and again at teatime. Teatime was the special family meal; she speaks very fondly of spending that time with her kids.

Elizabeth and Philip went on a royal tour in Paris in May of 1948, Elizabeth already pregnant and suffering from morning sickness, yet keeping it quiet until they could get home and make the formal announcement. Charles Philip Arthur George was born in November 1948 at Buckingham Palace with four doctors and one midwife in attendance, but no Prince Philip (not unusual for fathers of the time). He was playing squash in the other end of the Palace. When their son was born, her father, King George's press secretary, said, "I knew she'd do it! She'd never let us down." It seems that even in childbirth, the future Queen was getting it right. King George VI was "simply delighted," and Elizabeth herself said, "I still find it hard to believe that I really have a baby of my own," exactly like every new mother says when she has her first child. Elizabeth nursed the baby herself for the first two months until she contracted measles (a side effect of not going to public school as a child) and Charles had to be sent away temporarily to keep him healthy. Charles was cared for in infancy and childhood by two Scottish nannies and his own nursery footman whose job it was to maintain the royal baby carriage, among other things.

When Charles was born, Philip was still in active service in the Royal Navy, and Elizabeth was not yet Queen. Philip was soon posted to Malta, leaving as second-in-command on the HMS Chequers. Elizabeth wanted to be with him and certainly had the staff to watch the baby, so six days after Charles's first birthday, in November 1949, Elizabeth went to Malta for five weeks. Charles spent that Christmas with his grandparents at Sandringham, the royal estate in Norfolk. The future Queen had some royal duties, but mostly enjoyed the freedom and anonymity of life in Malta, living at the Mountbatten's villa, learning to ride side-saddle (a loathsome but necessary skill), driving around with Philip in his convertible, and learning her new favorite hobby--photography. Elizabeth

Philip had just returned from Malta when Anne Elizabeth Alice Louise was born at Clarence House in London in August 1950. Just a couple of months later, Elizabeth left again for Malta with Philip, the two children staying with their grandparents for another Christmas at Sandringham. King George and Queen Elizabeth were crazy about their grandchildren, spending a lot of time with them and getting to know them well. The next year after Elizabeth and Philip had been on tour in Canada and the United States, the couple returned three days after Charles's third birthday. Even though they had been gone a month, it was not an affectionate public reunion with the children at Euston Station. Elizabeth hugged her mother and Margaret and gave Charles a peck on the cheek, causing the press to write "Britain's heiress presumptive puts her duty first. Motherly love must await the privacy of Clarence House." Charles left the station with his grandparents, not his parents. Christmas of 1951 is the first year the family is all together for the holiday.

When the King dies in 1952, Elizabeth's life changes dramatically. Philip soon leaves the Navy, and the family moves from Clarence House to Buckingham Palace.

Elizabeth also gets a new private secretary, Martin Charteris, who stays with her for the next several decades.

Charteris is very good to Elizabeth and a better match for Philip—congenial, dedicated, kind, and great with Elizabeth's public affairs. It is also about this time that Philip takes over more of the management of the household, the children, and the royal estates, especially now that he is no longer working at the Admiralty. "Philip is terribly independent," says the Queen, and Philip comments, "I had to try to support the Queen as best I could without getting in the way. The difficulty was to find things that might be useful."

The popular view is that Philip was too harsh on the children and the Queen too lenient, but we're left to wonder how fair that view really is. It does seem, however, that Philip never really understood young Charles, thinking him too soft and awkward.

Yet Philip took an active role in raising him, choosing for Charles the same school in Scotland that he had gone to. Charles hated it and called it a prison sentence, but his dad said, "Children may be indulged at home, but school is expected to be a Spartan and disciplined experience in the process of developing in self-controlled, considerate and independent adults."

Young Princess Anne, however, was more athletic, intelligent and clever but not particularly academic, more self-confident than Charles, and excelled at horseback riding and sailing (she would later go on to earn an equestrian medal at the Olympics in Montreal in 1976).

She enjoyed her boarding school in Hampshire and didn't seem to suffer much from some detached parenting, saying in her later years, "as all mothers, she's put up with a lot, and we're still on speaking terms, so I think that's no mean feat."

Pamela Mountbatten, Elizabeth and Philip's cousin commented on the couple not sharing a bedroom, saying, "In England the upper class always have had separate bedrooms. You don't want to be bothered with snoring, or someone flinging a leg around.

Then when you are feeling cozy, you share your room sometimes. It is lovely to be able to choose." Along with separate bedrooms, Elizabeth took several years to focus on learning to be Queen, establishing herself as monarch before she had her last two children. Andrew Albert Christian Edward was born in February 1960, and Edward Antony Richard Louis was born in 1964. When she was pregnant with Andrew, Elizabeth told Charteris, "I am going to have a baby, which I have been trying to do for some time, and that means I won't be able to go to Ghana as arranged. I want you to go and explain the situation to President Nkrumah and tell him to keep his mouth shut." Except for expecting a baby, "Nothing, but nothing deflected her from duty," Elizabeth was off on royal tours again soon after Andrew, and then Edward was born. Those were also the only times she ever missed opening Parliament.

Either the break between the two sets of children, her slightly older years, or her growing confidence made Elizabeth a more relaxed parent with the last two children. "Goodness what fun it is to have a baby in the house again!" was Elizabeth's remark after Edward was born. She spent more time playing with the young children (the older two were off to boarding school already), also spending more time in the nursery.

The nanny for the two older children, Helen

Lightbody, turned out to be too much of a drill sergeant, Philip eventually got rid of her and replaced her with a more gently nanny that Elizabeth liked better and found less intimidating, Mabel Anderson. If the Queen of England found the previous nanny too intimidating, we have to wonder why she stuck around at all; the new nanny was a better fit for the family. Andrew and Edward considered Windsor their home, just as Elizabeth had, riding their bikes through the halls and running through the gardens. The whole family did much better at family togetherness, like most families, when they were on vacation. Balmoral and Sandringham became the places to play together like Elizabeth had with her parents and Margaret when she was a child.

The Royal Yacht Brittania was also a family favorite; often, when they were in Balmoral, they would cruise around the islands and enjoy the privacy and seclusion as a family.

As the Prince of Wales, Charles's future was decided by his parents. He would go to Cambridge to study then on to the Royal Naval College, like his father.

Charles found he liked Cambridge a whole lot better than he'd liked Gordonstoun. He and Anne also took on more royal duties as they got older, Charles saying, "I learnt the way a monkey learns-by watching its parents," making us ask how well he took to his royal duties. Anne proved herself up to the task, however, when she was the victim of an attempted kidnapping in 1974. A young man stopped her chauffeured car along the Mall, shot her driver, two policemen, and a journalist and tried to drag Anne out of the car. Her response while kicking at him was "not bloody likely." She received an award for bravery from Harold Wilson, the Prime Minister at the time, and carried on with her royal duties as if nothing had happened.

Charles's marriage caused a little more trouble (ok, a lot more) for his parents. Philip was against his choice of Diana Spencer, but when it came down to it, finally said, in essence, it was time to either marry her or get on with it.

Elizabeth disliked confrontation and was a great diplomat plus just a genuinely kind person, so she treated Diana well throughout the marriage and divorce, no matter what Diana might have said.

And even with all of the bad press, the Queen got at Diana's death (that's a story for another day), the family credits her with holding everyone together, for being the emotional foundation for her grandsons at the time. Even the press came around after her public address where she spoke fondly of Diana's love for her children and her charities and told the nation that she was speaking as "a queen and a grandmother" telling the public we should not judge the way someone else grieves.

It's true that Philip and Elizabeth's children have gotten some bad press over the years. Anne was known as "her royal rudeness" during the 80s. Then there's Charles and Diana while they were together after they separated, and then Charles and Camilla. There was a very ill-advised celebrity gameshow that Edward got Andrew and his wife Fergie to participate in, called It's a Royal Knockout. Plus Andrew and Fergie's divorce complete with photos of Fergie's new amour sucking on her toes. But through it all, while Philip in his natural way spoke up and out, Elizabeth kept her cool. She was kind to the divorcing couples (even allowing them to divorce, they can maybe thank Aunt Margaret for paving the way there) and kind and inclusive to the once-daughters-in-law. It is difficult, actually, to find the Queen saying an unkind word about any of them even though we have to assume that her children drove her crazy sometimes just as happens with the rest of us.

Andrew paid her a compliment in his older years, saying, "The Queen's intelligence network is a hell of a lot better than anyone's in this Palace. Bar none. She knows everything. I don't know how she does it. And she sees everything." While Charles seems willing to voice his criticism to the press freely sometimes, on the whole, the royal family seems to be very loyal to each other—maybe not affectionate but at least loving. Living her life publicly and raising her children in the spotlight would pose no end of difficulties for any of us. It was Anne who said of her mother something that more of us might hope our children would say: "I don't believe that any of us, for a second, though she didn't care for us in exactly the same way as any other mother did ... We've all been allowed to find our own way, and we were always encouraged to discuss problems, to talk them through. People have to make their own mistakes, and I think she's always accepted that."

THE QUEEN ON TOUR
ROYAL TOURS AND THE COMMONWEALTH

During her long reign, Queen Elizabeth has made more than 260 official overseas visits to over 116 countries around the world. She is the most traveled head of state by far. She is the first monarch to circle the globe yet she does not hold a passport—British passports are issued in the name of the Queen, so she really doesn't have any reason to issue one to herself in her own name, although the rest of the royal family have passports. She hardly needs an introduction when she travels, but years ago on a tour in Scotland, her host got tangled in his sword trying to get out of the car, so Elizabeth finally introduced herself, saying, "My Lord-Lieutenant appears to be having difficulty in getting out of the car, so I'd better introduce myself. I'm the Queen."

Elizabeth went on her first airplane flight in 1945, a trip to Northern Ireland with her parents. Six months later, she went on her first official visit without her parents.

Before her marriage to Philip, Elizabeth went on a royal tour to Africa with her sister Margaret and her parents, in 1947. The trip was a way to introduce Elizabeth to the Commonwealth, and while the month-long boat trip there and back was full of seasickness, the family had a wonderful time together as just "we four," as they liked to call themselves. Elizabeth got to see how her parents coped with the grueling schedule despite her father's failing health. She learned about race relations in South Africa and Rhodesia—knowledge and skills that would prove valuable to her later in her reign as these countries faced rebellions and unrest. In South Africa, Elizabeth celebrated her twenty-first birthday, with parties and a speech broadcast across the Commonwealth which she addressed to the young people who had suffered in the "terrible and glorious years of the second world war." She said for the first time what would become her message throughout her reign: "If we all go forward together with an unwavering faith, a high courage, and a quiet heart, we shall be able to make of this ancient Commonwealth an even grander thing--more free, more prosperous, more happy, and a more powerful influence for good in the world. I should like to make [a] dedication now. It is very simple. I declare before you all that my whole life whether it be long or short shall be devoted to your service and the service of our great imperial family to which we all belong."

Her father, King George VI, dedicated himself to the welfare of the Commonwealth, as well. The notion of the Commonwealth is a 20th-century invention to describe countries once in the Empire but now transitioning to independence while still keeping their link to the monarchy. No longer ruling colonies like in the 18th and 19th centuries or fighting the Spanish Armada and spreading across the world like Imperial Britain of the first Queen Elizabeth's reign, Queen Elizabeth II felt it was her duty to show compassion and guidance to the countries that once fell under Britain's rule. While she doesn't have executive power in the Commonwealth countries, she has a lot of influence, often being sent in (or choosing to send herself in) when she sees them needing a push in the right direction, or to pave the way for the Prime Minister to open discussions with their leaders. Philip calls her the "Commonwealth psychotherapist."

In 1951, before her accession to the throne, Elizabeth and Philip took a 35-day royal tour across Canada and the United States, learning their new roles as royal diplomats. Elizabeth told Charteris, her private secretary, "my face is aching from smiling." Philip, however, made a public joke about Canada being "a good investment" for the Crown.

That comment didn't get quite the same reception. Charteris explained it this way, saying Philip "was impatient. He hadn't yet defined his role . . . and sometimes, I think, felt that the Princess paid more attention to them than to him." One wonders how Philip thinks it could be otherwise. They would find their roles as the years went on, although Philip would still put his foot in his mouth fairly regularly. On a later tour of the Cayman Islands, Philip said, "aren't you all descended from pirates?" He also didn't suffer the press lightly, at one point responding to a question he didn't like with the remark, "damn fool question," and telling a group in the Caribbean, "you have mosquitos, I have the press."

And on one notable occasion when a member of the press asked how his flight was, Philip responded, "Have you ever flown in a plane?" "Oh yes sir, many times" "Well, it was just like that." Philip even had a name for it, given when he was speaking at a dental conference: "Dontopedalogy is the science of opening your mouth and putting your foot in it, a science which I have practiced a

HMY Britannia - Used on many tours

Elizabeth, on the other hand, rarely spoke a wrong word. When she visited Niagara Falls on the trip in 1951, she worried about the mist ruining her hair, saying "It looks very damp." And on a royal trip to Norway where she opened an art exhibition of giant nude sculptures, she said she made sure "I was not photographed between a pair of those great thighs." She was immensely popular on her royal tours, drawing huge crowds. On the trip to Washington in 1951, President Truman called her "a fairy princess," taken with her immediately. She had that effect on people. Plus she was dedicated, hard-working, and empathetic.

When a Canadian official thought Elizabeth might need a break, her secretary responded, "Her Majesty is trained for eight hours," and another staff member once said, "she's got very good legs, and she can stand for a long time ... The Queen is tough as a yak."

While Elizabeth refuses to give interviews to the press, she does show the same compassion and dedication to them as she does to everyone else. When a member of the press was traveling with her entourage on a royal tour, and his wife went into labor back in London, it was clear that the journalist wasn't going to make it home in time on a commercial flight, so the Queen said, "that won't do at all, let him fly home with me on my royal flight."

November 1953 saw the start of a 43,000-mile royal tour for Elizabeth and Philip from Bermuda west through the Panama Canal on to Fiji then New Zealand and Australia where Elizabeth was the first reigning monarch to visit. During the three weeks on the boat, Elizabeth worked in her office daily but also spent a lot of time playing on deck with Philip and the staff. In Fiji she was a good sport about eating strange foods, in Tonga she was reunited with Queen Salote who had come to her coronation and been very popular. Elizabeth was a good sport again in Tonga when she had to sit on the floor and eat with her hands. All over the Pacific, Philip and Elizabeth were crowd-pleasers. Philip said, "The level of adulation, you wouldn't believe it, it could have been corroding. It would have been very easy to play to the gallery, but I took a conscious decision not to do that. Safer not to be too popular. You can't fall too far." Philip was also a great consolation to Elizabeth when the schedule got too tough, telling her, "don't look so sad, sausage." The couple then continued on from Australia to Ceylon (Sri Lanka), Uganda, and Libya, where Elizabeth had a hard time with the heat (as anyone would). The newly-finished royal yacht which Philip had helped design, Brittania, met them in Libya, with young Charles and Anne on board.

After several months apart, the first reunion with the children was not as warm as Charles might have liked. Elizabeth had to greet the dignitaries on board first, telling Charles, "no, not you dear," something Charles would always remember. In private, however, the family had a great reunion, with Charles showing his parents all over the yacht that he'd already been traveling on for a week.

Philip goes on all of the royal tours with Elizabeth, the ones where he goes somewhere on his own raises eyebrows with the press and elicits comments about how their marriage must be in trouble. Elizabeth is always firm about how that is not the case.

Yet even when they are together, they sometimes fight like other couples. On one royal tour to Australia when the couple were heard fighting, Elizabeth later tells the staff, "I'm sorry for that little interlude, but as you know, it happens in every marriage." On a solo tour of Philip's in 1956 when he opened the Olympic Games in Melbourne and was gone for four months, rumors of trouble in the royal marriage were particularly rampant. To quell the gossip, Elizabeth and her staff met Philip on board the Brittania sporting false beards to match the ones Philip and the crew had grown.

On a royal tour to Canada in 1957, Elizabeth was the first monarch to open Canadian Parliament. She then went on to the U.S. to meet Eisenhower, who had been a great friend to her parents during World War II.

He went on to say, "You both have captivated the people of our country by your charm and graciousness."

She carried that graciousness on to a football game in Maryland (where she didn't understand the rules), and to an impromptu stop at a grocery store, where she commented to one mother shopping, "how nice that you can bring your children along." (She clearly didn't realize that most American moms would rather not bring their children along but rarely have a choice). The manager of the supermarket commented after she left, "it was the greatest thing that ever happened to me." Eisenhower later returned the visit with a visit of his own to Balmoral where Elizabeth cooked scones for him herself, sending him the recipe written by hand.

The Commonwealth was always very special to Elizabeth; she considers it her legacy. Countries that might have left the Commonwealth while in crisis stayed because of her influence. While on a royal tour to New Zealand in 1953, she gave her Christmas message from there, commenting "the Crown is not merely an abstract symbol of our unity but a personal and living bond between you and me." And in a Christmas message in 1957, Elizabeth addressed the Commonwealth, saying, "I cannot lead you into battle, but I can do something else. I can give you my heart, and my devotion to those old islands and to all the peoples of our brotherhood of nations." She had shown that devotion a year earlier in Nigeria, shaking hands with recovering lepers. In 1961 she went to Ghana to try to keep the country in the Commonwealth even though they had already declared their independence. It was a dangerous trip, not recommended by her advisers, but her response was, "How silly I should look if I was scared to visit Ghana and then Khrushchev went and had a good reception." The trip was a huge success and a great diplomatic move, Ghana stayed in the Commonwealth. Elizabeth made the first royal visit to Germany since World War II in 1965—Philip got to return to where he used to live with his sisters, and Elizabeth was cheered in the streets, although that made her uncomfortable, thinking it would remind people too much of a Nazi rally.

Elizabeth was the first to introduce the royal walkabout in Australia and New Zealand, where she wanders among the crowd meeting the locals, because as Elizabeth herself says, "I have to be seen to be believed." She was the first British monarch to visit China, traveling there in 1986. In 1991 on her third state visit to the United States, she was the first British monarch to address both houses of Congress.

In 2002, her Golden Jubilee year marking fifty years on the throne, she takes another royal tour around the Commonwealth, but by her Diamond Jubilee in 2012, she and Philip had started only going on "awaydays," tours in the United Kingdom, sending their children and grandchildren on the overseas tours. Elizabeth once said, "If I wore beige, no one would know who I am." As the world's most traveled monarch, now serving for over 66 years, she probably doesn't need to worry anymore about not being recognized anymore.

POLITICAL QUEEN

THE QUEEN AND HER PRIME MINISTERS

According to Victorian constitutionalist Walter Bagehot, "the sovereign has under a constitutional monarchy such as ours, three rights—the right to be consulted, the right to encourage, the right to warn."

Along with those rights, it used to be the Queen's prerogative to choose a Prime Minister and dissolve a parliament, technically speaking. In our day, however, she doesn't so much choose the Prime Minister as appoint or confirm one. And she no longer dissolves a government, either. Starting in 1922 for the Labour Party and 1965 for the Conservative Party, the party chooses their candidate for Prime Minister and sends the name on to the Queen so she can formally ask him to act as Prime Minister, a process which the Palace calls "You Choose, We Send For." And as for dissolving a government, that duty now falls to the majority in the House of Commons. Queen Elizabeth II is in the delicate position of complete political neutrality.

She is meant to reign, not rule, and just like Bagehot said, consult, encourage, and warn.

As we talked about in our discussion of Queen Elizabeth's childhood, Elizabeth was given a rigorous education on the constitution and the workings of the British government. On many occasions, the new Prime Minister has come in for his or her first weekly meeting with the Queen and been stunned by her knowledge of the constitution and what's happening in the country. They have also all, unanimously, commented on her ability to listen and counsel without getting too involved, thus maintaining her neutrality. While she has the power to veto a law passed by Parliament, she would never use it, considering that too political. She is, however, consulted on or at least informed of the daily happenings in the government, fastidiously reading through her official red boxes every day.

As the Head of the Church of England, the Queen also appoints the Archbishop of Canterbury. She does this about the same way as choosing the Prime Minister—a name is brought to her, she discusses it with the Prime Minister, and she makes the appointment.

That process does not, however, mean she has no pull in the decision. Prime Ministers often comment that if the Queen doesn't quite agree

The Queen's Prime Ministers

- Winston Churchill, 1951-55
- Anthony Eden, 1955-57
- Harold Macmillan, 1957-63
- Alec Douglas-Home, 1963-64
- Harold Wilson, 1964-70, 1974-76
- Edward Heath, 1970-74
- James Callaghan, 1976-79
- Margaret Thatcher, 1979-1990
- John Major, 1990-97
- Tony Blair, 1997-2007
- Gordon Brown, 2007-10
- David Cameron, 2010-16
- Theresa May, 2016-2019
- Boris Johnson, 2019-Present

with their suggestion, in this or other matters, she asks questions, has a discussion, and listens patiently, "It's a very subtle way of making the Prime Minister think again." Just as she does in matters of the Commonwealth, she is meant to soothe ruffled feathers, listen, and encourage.

Queen Elizabeth's first Prime Minister was Winston Churchill, now in his second round as PM. He was a great start for her reign--he had been her father's Prime Minister and ally during the War, he had been at her wedding and had met her for the first time when she was just two years old. Churchill and Elizabeth were very fond of each other. She later said of him that none "will ever, for me, be able to hold the place of my first Prime Minister," but she also found him "very obstinate" (didn't everybody?). They did have a great shared history, though, and a common love of horses. She learned a lot from his guidance in her early years, and he was quickly impressed with her sharp intelligence and command of the intricacies of governing. Churchill's health was declining, however, suffering two strokes while in office under her reign. He dragged his feet on retiring, and Elizabeth didn't want to push him too hard.

He did finally retire as Prime Minister in 1955,

saying he wanted to die there. He almost got his wish, passing just a year later. While still in office as PM, he was knighted by the Queen, an honor that not all Prime Ministers receive, and upon his retirement, the Queen offered him a Dukedom, something reserved for royalty. She was confident, however, in offering this honor, knowing that he would never accept it. Luckily she bet correctly. She did, however, give him an elaborate state funeral at St. Paul's "to acknowledge our debt of gratitude for the life and example of a national hero."

Elizabeth's next Prime Minister was Anthony Eden, who had to resign after just two years because of his rather shifty involvement in the Suez Canal crisis, angering Eisenhower, the United Nations, and some Commonwealth nations as well as a lot of the British population who had thought he was pursuing diplomatic avenues to solve the crisis while he was actually sending in British troops to invade Egypt. Eden did, however, keep the Queen informed of his decisions and plans even though she couldn't do much to stop him; this was the first time she saw classified government documents, but it would not be the last and proved to be a good education for her later during Margaret Thatcher's tenure and the Falkland Islands invasion.

Harold Macmillan, the Queen's next Prime Minister, was notable for his involvement in Elizabeth's family affairs. The two got along well, him calling her "a great support because she is the one person you can talk to." It was Macmillan who took on the task of making Philip happier about his position in the family. Philip was still smarting about not being able to hand his last name down to his children and was still trying to find his place in the royal duties. Macmillan visited Elizabeth at Sandringham, the family estate in Norfolk, in January of 1960 to discuss the last name dilemma. He later commented, "What upsets me is the Prince's almost brutal attitude to the Queen over all this." To soothe the issue, the Prime Minister suggested that any grandchildren of the Queen who did not hold the title of Royal Highness (therefore not in direct line for the throne) would be given the last name of Mountbatten-Windsor, a suggestion that appeased Philip, along with the Prime Minister's suggestion to make Philip a prince

of the realm. Macmillan managed to suggest some truly useful solutions for the Queen's personal life. Their friendship would continue long after he left his post as Prime Minister.

The first time Queen Elizabeth seemed to not get along with one of her Prime Ministers was when Edward Heath became her sixth PM. Heath was brusque, misogynistic, and humorless, and worst of all, he treated the Queen's beloved Commonwealth badly. In 1971, Heath banned Elizabeth from attending the Commonwealth Leaders meeting in Singapore, thinking she was too much of an interference and a distraction. The Queen was livid. She was Head of the Commonwealth and felt a great deal of sympathy for those countries. Later, Heath also tried to censor the Queen's remarks when miners in Britain went on strike as a result of his progressive socialist policies. Elizabeth responded to the troubles in the country his policies brought on—high unemployment, riots, inflation—in her Christmas broadcast of 1973: "Let us remember, however, that what we have in common is more important than what divides us." Heath's biggest success was Britain's entry into the European Common Market (later called the European Economic Community), but this was done with the Queen's help as well. Heath's application to the Common Market was the country's third try; the Queen had been instrumental in wooing the French over the years when Heath and previous Prime Ministers had applied.

Margaret Thatcher turned out to be a trickier Prime Minister for the Queen than either of them might have expected. The two of them might have formed an immediate bond as two women of such close age in rare positions of power. However, the two had such different personalities that the bond took years to form. Lucky for them, Thatcher was Elizabeth's longest-serving Prime Minister, so they had plenty of time to perfect their relationship. Thatcher was trying to get the nation back on track after years of economic downturn and unrest; she was tough and no-nonsense, earning herself the name "Iron Lady." Elizabeth felt that at their weekly meetings, Thatcher lectured instead of listened: "Mrs. Thatcher never listens to a word I say." And their differences were in sharpest contrast when Thatcher came on her yearly visit to Balmoral, the Queen's vast estate in Scotland.

Thatcher found these visits too informal, especially the family picnic where Philip grills and Elizabeth does the clearing up, causing the Queen to remark, "will someone please tell that woman to sit down." And on the long rambles that Elizabeth likes to take around the estate when Thatcher couldn't keep up, the Queen was heard to say, "I think you'll find Mrs. Thatcher only walks on the road." Queen Elizabeth and Mrs. Thatcher were both uncomfortable with each other at Balmoral

The two worked as a great team, however, when the country required it. When several countries in Africa were considering leaving the Commonwealth because Rhodesia was trying to gain a black majority in their government, the Queen went and did what she does best—calming people down so the government could get to work. After her visit, Rhodesia claimed its independence as the Republic of Zimbabwe, and several countries, including Rhodesia, stayed in the Commonwealth, which was exactly what Elizabeth and Thatcher were hoping for. As one adviser put it, "The fact that she was there made it happen." In 1982 when Argentina invaded the Falkland Islands, a British territory since the 1700s, Margaret Thatcher sent in British troops, including the Queen's son, Prince Andrew. Andrew was a helicopter pilot, and while the government didn't think the second in line to the throne should be in a war zone, the Queen fully supported him, thereby also lending her support to the war and the Commonwealth. Thatcher said during this crisis, "We have ceased to be a nation in retreat," proving that Britain was back on track and gaining strength.

By the time Thatcher left office, Queen Elizabeth was a big fan, honoring her with the Order of the Garter, which most Prime Ministers receive, but also the more rare Order of Merit, just as she'd given to Churchill and Macmillan.

Tony Blair was the Queen's first Prime Minister to be born after her accession to the throne. As somewhat of a youngster, he had a harder time relating to the life of the royalty and was sometimes unsure of the need for a monarch. And still, he gave her a glowing compliment at a Palace function, calling her "a symbol of unity in a world of insecurity . . . Simply the best of British." Blair became an integral part of the royal family's image upon the death of the Queen's former daughter-in-law, Diana. Blair knew Diana rather well when he took the post of Prime Minister, which put him in a unique position to help out in the crisis that was Diana's death. Blair had been fairly vocal about Diana's dangerous relationship with the press after her divorce, sharing some of the same feelings as the Queen even if she couldn't voice them publicly. But when Diana was killed in a car crash in 1997, just at the start of Blair's tenure, Blair was instrumental in helping the Queen preserve her image as she was criticized by the press. At the time of the accident, the Queen was in Balmoral, far from London, with Diana's children Harry and William. She chose to keep the children out of the mayhem and media circus in London to allow them time to grieve as a family before returning. That decision was met with heaps of criticism in the press and a public outcry, with people thinking that meant the Queen didn't care.

Blair, Prince Charles, and the Palace advisers managed the crisis in London, showing great ingenuity, flexibility, and sympathy. Upon the Queen's return to the Palace, when she gave a touching speech about grief and Diana's best qualities, Blair publicly praised her, saying, "she managed to be Queen and a grandmother at one and the same time."

All of her many Prime Ministers comment on Queen Elizabeth's intelligence and command of her tasks; she impresses them all and manages to make each of them comfortable, offering "friendliness, not friendship," which seems just about the right fit for a monarch and her Prime Minister. In the words of a former leader of the House of Lords, "She makes dictatorship more difficult, she makes military coups more difficult, rule by decree more difficult. It is more difficult because she occupies space, and due process must be followed." As her admittedly favorite Prime Minister, Winston Churchill, said, "A great battle is lost: Parliament turns out the government. A great battle is won: crowds cheer the Queen." This seems to be her great gift, that even while Prime Ministers come and go, she is always there, that she unifies the people.

THE QUEEN'S BOAT

A Visit to HMY Britannia

By Jonathan Thomas

We knew pretty early on that when we visited Edinburgh, the one thing we had to see was the Royal Yacht Britannia. It's now the most popular tourist attraction in Scotland, and people quite enjoy poking around what used to be a very personal space for HM The Queen and the Royal Family. The yacht itself has a fascinating history - and its current status (and the desire to commission a new one) has become symbolic of Brexit Britain. When we visited, it was early in the day, and it was nice and sunny. The perfect day to explore an important ship.

The Royal Family travels in style wherever they go, and their conveyances include coaches, Rolls Royce, Land Rovers, a Sikorsky helicopter, an RAF Airbus, and even their own fabulous yacht—the Britannia. Colloquially known as the Royal Yacht Britannia, its official designation is Her Majesty's Yacht (HMY) Britannia (not HMS, these things are important to pedants), and it has a long and storied history with the Royal Family. Britannia was in service from 1954 until 1997 and has not been replaced since it was retired. It was not, however, the first Royal Yacht.

The first Royal Yacht was the HMY Mary in 1660. She was the first ship of her kind in the Royal Navy and was constructed by the Dutch East India Company for King Charles II, a gift from the Dutch government celebrating the Restoration of the English throne after the English Civil Wars. Charles only used her for a year before he commissioned a faster ship and relegated the Mary to diplomatic voyages. Other royal yachts before the Britannia have included the William and Mary, the Royal George, the Royal Charlotte, and at least three iterations of the Victoria and Albert, amongst others. Several battleships have also been used to transport the Royal Family over the past century, with the last notable ship being the HMS Vanguard in 1947.

The Britannia's immediate predecessor was the Victoria & Albert III. It was built for Queen Victoria and was the first Royal Yacht not to be powered entirely by sails. Interestingly, Victoria never set foot on it as she didn't consider it stable, but her son, King Edward VII, made use of it during his reign.

The Britannia was the last ship in this proud tradition. Its construction was ordered on February 5, 1952, and the firm responsible was John Brown & Co. Ltd in Scotland (the Scottish connections

of the ship dictate why its current home is now Edinburgh). Working from their shipyards in Clydebank, Dunbartonshire, the firm designed it to have three masts (a foremast, mainmast, and mizzenmast), with the aerials on the foremast and the mainmast on hinges so that the Britannia could go under bridges. The ship was capable of 12,000 horsepower and a speed of up to 22.5 knots. In case of another war, the ship was also designed to be converted into a hospital ship. The keel was laid down in June 1952, and it was the last fully-riveted ship to have a smooth painted hull. The ship's name was a closely-guarded secret until Queen Elizabeth II launched the Britannia on April 16, 1953 (named for Britain's mythical national personification).

At the launch of Britannia, Empire wine was used to commission the ship rather than champagne as post-War Britain was still experiencing shortages, and champagne was deemed too extravagant for the occasion.

HMY Britannia's maiden voyage took place starting on April 14, 1954, transporting the very young Prince Charles and Princess Anne to meet their parents at the end of the Queen and Duke of Edinburgh's Commonwealth Tour. The Royal Family then embarked together for the first time on May 1, 1954. Of course, the Britannia wasn't for the sole use of Queen Elizabeth and Prince Phillip. Over its decades of service, the ship sometimes served as a love boat for newly-minted Royal couples, ferrying them on their honeymoons, beginning with Princess Margaret and Anthony Armstrong-Jones in 1960. It played host to a number of US Presidents such as Dwight D. Eisenhower, Gerald Ford, and Bill Clinton.

Some of the Royal touches in the ship included a grand staircase for greeting guests that also included the likes of Prime Minister Winston Churchill, comedian Noel Coward, and South African President Nelson Mandela.

Besides shepherding the Royals all over the world, the Britannia had a number of roles unrelated to its original purpose. The Britannia sometimes traveled the globe as a representative for British business, pulling into port and inviting CEOs from multiple nations to tour and experience its luxury for themselves. Known as "Sea Days," these voyages proved to be very profitable for the British government, and the Overseas Trade Board estimated that the Britannia made roughly £3 billion for the Exchequer between 1991 and 1995

alone. During the civil war in Yemen in 1986, the Britannia was pressed into service as a rescue ship, evacuating British nationals and others. It was able to enter the country's waters without potentially causing an international incident due to its status as a non-combatant vessel.

The Britannia was the only ship in the Royal Navy to have a laundry service permanently onboard, as Officers and Yachtsmen sometimes had to change uniform six times a day based on the conditions of the voyage.

Unfortunately, all good things come to an end. During the Conservative government of Prime Minister John Major, HMY Britannia determined that a refit to continue its use would cost £17 million. Major's government proposed commissioning a new Royal Yacht if needed in 1997, but the announcement so close to a general election may have been one of the factors in electing Tony Blair's "New Labour" government. The new Labour government would not commit to a replacement during the first two years and ultimately opted not to replace the ship. Its last diplomatic voyage served to ferry Hong Kong's last governor, Chris Patten, and Prince Charles back to the United Kingdom following the transfer of the island to the Republic of China in 1997.

The Queen is not known to be overly emotional in person or in private, but when she was at the decommissioning ceremony, you can see her visibly cry. The Queen loved Britannia; it was her private home - her private bit of Britain - wherever they went around the globe. The crews catered to their every whim, and when they were at sea - sometimes for months at a time when on Royal Tours - it was a very private place. Some of her happiest memories were there. When you tour the vessel, you get the impression that you're visiting a very personal place. There is no shortage of Royal Palaces in Britain, but they're rather grand affairs - that dwarf the human scale. The Royal Yacht was a functional Royal Palace-on-sea that reflected austerity Britain, the era in which it was built. It's not grand - in fact, it's rather shabby - especially after years of sitting aside a dock.

It is now listed as part of the National Historic Fleet (meaning it has special protections and regulations for its continued maintenance). Britannia as a visitor attraction moored in the historic Port of Leith in Edinburgh, Scotland, and is cared for by the Royal Yacht Britannia Trust, a registered charity whose sole purpose is to preserve the ship. There was some controversy in the siting of the ship - many believe that it should be located on the Clyde where she was built. But Edinburgh was considered the most likely place to attract the most tourists.

The ship is rather well preserved in aspic - much as it was when the Queen last used it. The rooms are rather large and impressive, considering they're on a small ship. Anyone who's been on another ship like the Queen Mary would be impressed. We quite liked our visit to the ship - which included a spot of 'proper' tea in the onsite cafe, which gives you views of the ship and the surrounding port. One cannot help but feel a faded sense of grandeur.

Which is a feeling you often get throughout Britain but is perhaps something you notice only after repeated visits. The fate of the Britannia has become another controversy in the department that is the endless war over Brexit. The current Conservative government, as of this writing, is proposing to commission a new Royal Yacht that would sail the seven seas again band become a symbol of the 'newly vibrant and free' post-Brexit Britain and drum up crucial business and free trade deals. A new symbol of Britain's soft power. The problem is that the idea is laughable in Britain's current cultural climate. The Royal Family has privately made it very clear they have no desire for another ship. The British public has no desire to spend hundreds of millions of pounds on a white elephant ship in a time of pandemic enforce austerity. The Royal Navy would rather not have to staff a ship of that size and run it.

Boris Johnson may very well get his way - he always seems to do so.

Still as an outside observer, and after having toured Britannia and gotten a sense of how things used to be for the Royal Family and Britain, one rather thinks that it might be kind of nice for a new Royal Yacht and a new generation of Royals to spread Britain's culture across the world. Still, I doubt they'll even build it. This idea is mooted every few years and dismissed in a news cycle or two. But it's not an idea that ever really goes away.

THE ABDICATION CRISIS

CHOOSING LOVE OVER DUTY

If there was a trilogy of movies about the Queen's life made, this would be the prequel because, without it, she would never have been anywhere near the throne. In 1936, the charismatic new King, Edward VIII, announced to his advisors his intention of marrying his mistress, Wallis Simpson. Not since Henry VIII resolved to marry Anne Boleyn had a royal marriage threatened to wreak such havoc on the country. Henry was able to force his will on the kingdom. Four hundred years later, Edward found that his personal desires were no match for the State's, and he was obliged to abdicate, opening the way for a new royal family who would endear themselves to the nation.

A Burden Too Heavy Without the Help and Support of the Woman He Loved

Edward, known as David to his family and friends, was born on 23 June, 1894. His great-grandmother, Queen Victoria, was still on the throne, and his grandfather, Edward, Prince of Wales, was waiting impatiently in the wings. Young Edward's parents were the Duke and Duchess of York, who would later become King George V and Queen Mary.

As a child, Edward enjoyed an affectionate, albeit distant, relationship with his parents and grandparents. He was taught by tutors until his early teens, when he was sent first to Osborne Naval College and then Dartmouth Naval College to prepare him for a career in the Royal Navy. This plan was cut short in 1910 when his grandfather died. 16-year-old Edward was created Prince of Wales and sent to Magdalen College, Oxford, to better prepare him for his role as future King. His academic career was not a great success; whilst he enjoyed the University's polo club, he did not manage to attain a degree.

At the outbreak of the Great War, the Prince of Wales was determined to serve his country. He had joined the Grenadier Guards and appealed to be allowed to join the front line. His request was turned down since the government could not countenance the risk of the heir to the throne being captured by the enemy. Edward was allowed to serve behind the lines and occasionally managed to reach the front. Later, he flew military aircraft. Unlike the government, he was sanguine about the dangers and was

Key Dates

- January 1931 First meeting of Prince of Wales and Mrs. Wallis Simpson
- 20 January 1936   Death of George V. Edward VIII succeeds him
- July 1936   Mr. Simpson leaves the family home
- August 1936 Foreign newspapers print photographs of the King and Wallis
- 27 October 1936 Simpsons granted a decree nisi
- November 1936   The King informs Prime Minister he wants a morganatic marriage
- November 1936   King's proposal rejected by governments of Britain and Dominions
- 2 December 1936   King informed of the decision
- 3 December 1936   British Press break the story, and Mrs. Simpson leaves for France
- 9 December 1936   Edward tells government he intends to abdicate
- 10 December 1936 Instrument of Abdication signed and House of Commons informed
- 11 December 1936 Edward broadcasts his decision to the nation
- 12 December 1936 Edward's brother Albert proclaimed as King George VI
- 12 December 1936 Edward, now Duke of Windsor, travels to Austria
- 3 June 1937 Edward and Wallis Simpson marry in France

said to have quipped, "What difference does it make if I am killed? The King has three other sons!" This carefree attitude won him a good deal of popularity among the troops, who were proud of the Prince who won the Military Cross.

Following the war, Edward traveled around Britain and the Empire as his father's representative. Good looking, sporty, and unattached, he became a favorite with photographers and gossip columnists, achieving celebrity status. Unlike his stern parents, he was affable and suited the modernity of the "roaring twenties ." The people may have loved his personality, but his character was giving his parents,

Key Figures

- Edward, Prince of Wales, briefly King of the United Kingdom and Dominions, Emperor of India, later Duke of Windsor.
- Bessie Wallis Warfield, later Wallis Spencer, then Wallis Simpson, and finally, Wallis, Duchess of Windsor.
- King George V
- Queen Mary
- Stanley Baldwin, Prime Minister
- Prince Albert, Duke of York, later King George VI
- Elizabeth, Duchess of York, later Queen Elizabeth

and their advisors cause for concern.

Edward, rather like his grandfather and namesake Edward VII, had grown into a womanizer. His affairs with married women appalled his strait-laced father, who began to favor his second son, the quiet and respectably married Albert. King George went so far as to declare that he hoped Edward never had children so that Albert and his wife could eventually succeed to the throne. The King also predicted that Edward would ruin himself within a year of his father's death. In 1931, Edward met the woman who would turn George V's hopes and fears into reality.

Wallis Simpson was a vivacious and charming American socialite, possessed a quick wit, effortless elegance, and, according to some, endless ambition. Early in 1931, Wallis and Edward met for the first time at a dinner party hosted by Edward's mistress, Lady Furness. Over the next few years, Edward and Mrs. Simpson chanced upon each other at society events. Edward developed a fascination with the charming American, and it is likely that the pair became lovers when Lady Furness was abroad in 1934. Part of Wallis's attraction for the Prince was her lack of deference to his position, and he was soon besotted.

Mrs. Simpson had captured the heart of the world's most eligible bachelor, but it was never likely that she would capture his crown. Wallis was entirely unsuitable as a queen consort. Even putting aside the malicious gossip about her earlier scandalous escapades in the Far East, there was the fact that she was a divorcee. As a rule, a divorcee like Wallis would not be allowed at court, much less allowed to marry the monarch. The growing relationship between the Prince of Wales and Wallis was viewed with alarm by the King, many of the Prince's old friends, and the government. Special Branch trailed the couple, reporting back on alleged liaisons between Wallis and other men, in the hope that a wedge could be driven between the pair. Their attempts were unsuccessful. The Prince's infatuation continued unabated and began to impact his official duties. Worse was to come.

King George V died on 20 January 1936, and Edward became King Edward VIII. He and Wallis watched from a window at St James' Palace as the proclamation was read. It was a clear indication that he wanted Wallis by his side. Although the country at large remained unaware of the King's affair, to his family, the court, and government, the unthinkable became obvious: Edward intended to marry Mrs. Simpson. Such a marriage was fraught with difficulty, largely because the monarch was the Supreme Head of the Church of England, and the Church did not allow the remarriage of divorced people whose spouses were living. Edward and Wallis plowed on with their plans. Wallis sued for divorce on the grounds of her husband's adultery and was granted a decree nisi in October 1936. In Edward's mind, one hurdle to his marriage had been crossed. He turned his attention to the next and came up with a plan he felt would answer his critics.

In November 1936, Edward met his Prime Minister, Stanley Baldwin, and suggested that he might contract a morganatic marriage with Wallis. This type of marriage would allow Edward to retain the crown, but Wallis would not become Queen, instead having a courtesy title. Any children of the marriage would be excluded from the line of succession. There was no precedent for such an arrangement in Britain though morganatic marriages were not unheard of in other European kingdoms. Baldwin told the King that he doubted that the people would accept a marriage to Mrs. Simpson but undertook to put the King's proposal to the government of Britain and her Dominions.

Baldwin put three alternatives to the various governments: that the King should be allowed to marry Mrs. Simpson and she become Queen; that the King marry Mrs. Simpson in a morganatic marriage or; the King abdicated the throne. With the

INSTRUMENT OF ABDICATION.

      I, Edward the Eighth, of Great Britain, Ireland, and the British Dominions beyond the Seas, King, Emperor of India, do hereby declare My irrevocable determination to renounce the Throne for Myself and for My descendants, and My desire that effect should be given to this Instrument of Abdication immediately.

      In token whereof I have hereunto set My hand this tenth day of December, nineteen hundred and thirty six, in the presence of the witnesses whose signatures are subscribed.

SIGNED AT
FORT BELVEDERE
IN THE PRESENCE
OF

Edward R I

Albert

Henry

George

exception of New Zealand's Prime Minister, who felt that the morganatic marriage proposal might work, the first two proposals were rejected. Mrs. Simpson was seen as an entirely unsuitable spouse for the King. In Britain, the leaders of the opposition parties also agreed that there could be no marriage between Mrs. Simpson and a reigning King. Winston Churchill was hopeful that if the matter could be delayed, the King would simply fall out of love with Wallis. Baldwin was not in favor of delay, wanting a swift resolution to the crisis.

As news spread about the King and Mrs. Simpson, Edward was not entirely without sympathizers. An unlikely alliance of politicians supported him, ranging from Oswald Mosely and his Union of Fascists to the Communist Party. Winston Churchill was rumored to be leading the King's supporters, but this was pure speculation. In the Press, and, therefore, the country, opinion was split. Broadly, the Establishment and the middle-class were against Edward's marriage to Mrs. Simpson, whilst progressives and the working class were more tolerant of the idea. Perhaps buoyed by his supporters, Edward made a last-ditch attempt to keep his crown and the woman he loved.

At the beginning of December, he drafted a speech in which he put his idea of a morganatic marriage to the public, making it clear that he would prefer to stay on the throne. The government blocked him from broadcasting the speech, citing constitutional difficulties. Edward bowed to the inevitable; it was Wallis or the crown, and there was no possibility of reconciling the two. He agreed to abdicate.

On 10 December 1936, Edward signed the abdication documentation with his three younger brothers as witnesses. His brother Albert became monarch, taking the regnal name George. The following day, announced as Prince Edward, he addressed the nation, telling the people that he could not carry out the heavy burden of responsibility without the support of the woman he loved.

Edward and Wallis Simpson married the following year in France. As the Duke and Duchess of Windsor, they enjoyed a lavish lifestyle, although they did court controversy for their apparent sympathy for the Nazi regime. Edward died in 1972 and was buried in the Royal Mausoleum at Frogmore. The Duchess died in 1986 and was buried with her husband.

Legacy

The abdication of Edward VIII cleared the way for George VI, the result that George V had always wanted. Although George VI was a shy man, he and his wife, Queen Elizabeth, provided the country with a calm stability during World War II and the Blitz in particular. George VI also presided over the dismantling of the British Empire and, like his daughter, Elizabeth II, proved to be a popular monarch providing a steady influence in difficult times.

Sites to visit

- Fort Belvedere in Windsor Great Park was Edward's country home, given to him by his father. Edward and Wallis spent time here together, and part of the television series Edward and Mrs. Simpson was filmed in the house. It was at Belvedere that Edward signed his abdication documents. The house is currently leased to private tenants, but it is occasionally open to raise money for charities.
- The Duke and Duchess of Windsor are buried at Frogmore Mausoleum, which is located in the Home Park of Windsor Castle. Frogmore House, gardens, and the Mausoleum are open to the public on a very limited basis. The annual timetable for opening can be found on the Royal Collection Trust's website.
- The State Rooms at Buckingham Palace are open for tours, making the public more welcome than Mrs. Simpson once was!

Film and TV

- In 1981, Edward Fox and Cynthia Harris starred as Edward and Mrs. Simpson in Thames Television's drama series. Available on DVD.
- Wallis And Edward (2006) stars Joely Richardson and Stephen Campbell Moore. Available on DVD or to rent from LoveFilm.
- The events were also depicted heavily in Netflix's The Crown.
- The events also play heavily into the plot of The King's Speech.

TOP 10 MOMENTS OF ELIZABETH'S LIFE AND REIGN

From the beginning, the unexpected has pervaded the 60-year reign of Queen Elizabeth II. As a child, "Lilibet" and her younger sister Margaret were groomed for a life considered ordinary by royal standards. However, at the age of 10, Elizabeth Alexandra Mary Windsor's future as Defender of the Faith was sealed when her father took the throne in an unforeseen turn of events (see the previous article about the abdication crisis). It would be the first of many detours along the royal road ahead. Here are the ten most important moments of her life and reign.

1. THE ABDICATION OF KING EDWARD VIII

When Elizabeth's grandfather King George V died in 1936, the crown passed to her uncle King Edward VIII. However, Edward refused to forsake plans to marry the twice-divorced American Wallis Simpson, opting instead to abdicate the throne less than a year after his father's death. The switch propelled her father, George VI, to the throne and altered Elizabeth's life forever. Suddenly the 10-year-old girl was reading the latest political news and absorbing lessons on British government.

2. ACCESSION TO THE THRONE

On February 6, 1952, while on a trip to Kenya with her husband, Prince Philip, Elizabeth learned her father had died, and she had inherited the crown at the age of 25. She immediately returned to Britain as quickly as possible. Thrust into the global spotlight, Elizabeth was named Time Magazine's Woman of the Year – 1952.

3. CORONATION

Elizabeth's coronation as Queen at Westminster Abbey on June 2, 1953, was the first coronation broadcast on television. The more than 8,000 guests, including prime ministers and other heads of state from throughout the Commonwealth, witnessed the Archbishop of Canterbury place the crown on her head. In a radio broadcast marking the occasion, the Queen said, "throughout all my life and with all my heart, I shall strive to be worthy of

your trust."

4. SILVER JUBILEE – 1977

More than one million people gathered along the streets of London to watch the Royal Family, led by the Queen and Prince Philip in the golden state coach, on its way to St. Paul's at the launch of the Queen's Silver Jubilee celebrations.

"I want to thank all those in Britain and the Commonwealth who, through their loyalty and friendship, have given me strength and encouragement during these last 25 years," said the Queen at the time.

5. "ANNUS HORRIBILIS"

In a speech given November 24, 1992, to mark the 40th anniversary of her accession, the Queen referred to 1992 as her "annus horribilis," or horrible year. It was, after all, the year her sons Prince Charles and Andrew, the Duke of York, separated from their wives, Diana and Sarah, respectively; daughter Princess Anne divorced, and a fire destroyed a portion of Windsor Castle.

During that speech, Elizabeth said, "1992 is not a year on which I shall look back with undiluted pleasure. … I sometimes wonder how future generations will judge the events of this tumultuous year. I dare say that history will take a slightly more moderate view than that of some contemporary commentators."

6. DEATH OF DIANA, PRINCESS OF WALES

When Diana, former wife of Prince Charles, died following a car crash on August 31, 1997, members of the Royal Family were depicted as unemotional and lacking in compassion for not displaying grief publicly.

The Queen subsequently broke convention by bowing to Diana's coffin as it passed Buckingham Palace during the funeral procession and paid tribute to Diana during a live television broadcast

on September 9, 1997, thereby ending criticism from the tabloids.

During her speech, Elizabeth said, "Since last Sunday's dreadful news, we have seen, throughout Britain and around the world, an overwhelming expression of sadness at Diana's death. We have all been trying in our different ways to cope. It is not easy to express a sense of loss since the initial shock is often succeeded by a mixture of other feelings: disbelief, incomprehension, anger, and concern for those who remain. We have all felt those emotions in the last few days. So what I say to you now, as your Queen and as a grandmother, I say from my heart. First, I want to pay tribute to Diana myself. She was an exceptional and gifted human being. In good times and bad, she never lost her capacity to smile and laugh, nor to inspire others with her warmth and kindness. I admired and respected her for her energy and commitment to others, and especially for her devotion to her two boys."

7. THE DEATHS OF PRINCESS MARGARET AND THE QUEEN MOTHER

In 2002, the Queen lost her sister and only sibling, Princess Margaret, and her mother, the Queen Mother.

Margaret died on February 9. In a statement from the Palace, the Queen announced her death "with great sadness."

The Queen Mother died the following month on March 30 at the age of 101 with Elizabeth at her bedside.

8. RECEPTION FOR CHARLES AND CAMILLA

Despite her well-known disapproval of their relationship, the Queen held a reception at Windsor Castle in honor of the April 9, 2005 marriage of Prince Charles and Camilla Parker Bowles. She and Philip did not attend the civil

wedding ceremony. The marriage was said to have been the culmination of the long and controversial relationship of Charles and Camilla, the Duchess of Cornwall. Camilla has since grown on the Queen, and in celebration of the Platinum Jubilee, the Queen made it known that she would like Camilla to be considered Queen when Charles takes the throne.

9. ADVISING PRINCE WILLIAM ON HIS WEDDING

The Queen assisted her grandson in planning his April 29, 2011, wedding to Kate Middleton. Not only did Elizabeth advise William regarding what to wear (his Irish Guards uniform), she helped shape the guestlist for the marriage of the Duke and Duchess of Cambridge. "I rang her up and said 'Do we need to be doing this?' " he said in an article printed in The Daily Mail. "And she said, 'No. Start with your friends first and then go from there.' And she told me to bin the list."

10. FAREWELL TOUR, VISIT TO IRELAND

Last year, at the age of 85, the Queen embarked on what many referred to as her "Farewell Tour" of the Australia, her 16th visit to the continent.

She also became the first monarch to visit the Republic of Ireland since it gained independence in the 1920s. The historic four-day visit was conducted in May 2011; the Royal Family has since made several official visits to the Republic since.

BALMORAL
The Queen's Scottish Bolthole

Balmoral Castle will forever be known as the happy family home of Queen Victoria, Prince Albert, and their nine children. An epic Scotch Baronial castle, fit for the Queen of Great Britain and grandmother of Europe, Balmoral Castle remains the autumnal residence of the Royal family to this day. It is one of the Queen's favorite homes and considered the place where the Royal Family lets their hair down. It's considered a great honor to be invited to visit.

BRIEF FACTS ABOUT BALMORAL CASTLE

- Balmoral Castle is located in Royal Deeside, Aberdeenshire, Scotland.
- The current Balmoral Castle was built in 1856.
- The first Balmoral Castle was built in 1390 but was demolished in 1856 once the new Castle was complete.
- Balmoral estate was purchased by Prince Albert, Consort to Queen Victoria in 1852, and the house and estate remain the property of the royal family.

A BRIEF HISTORY OF BALMORAL CASTLE

On a flat expanse of meadowland on the south bank of the River Dee, 50 miles west of Aberdeen, sits Balmoral Castle. King Robert II of Scotland was the first monarch to be wooed by this patch of land having a hunting lodge built here in the 14th century but is by no means the last as Balmoral has been one of the private residences of the British royal family since 1852.

The first reference to a castle at Balmoral appears in 1452, referred to as 'Bouchmorale.' In 1539, the Castle appears again under the tenancy of Alexander and John Gordon, sons of the 1st Earl of Huntly, who added a tower house to the existing structure. The Castle was inherited by Anne Farquharson, wife of Charles Farquharson, a Jacobite who fought in the battle of Killiecrankie. Following the battle of Falkirk of 1746, where Farquharson's nephew James earned his name as

'Balmoral the Brave,' the Castle was forfeited and bought by the Earl of Fife. The lease next passed to Sir Robert Gordon, brother of the Prime Minister Earl of Aberdeen, who set about adding a major extension to the Castle, designed by John Smith of Aberdeen.

One morning, so the story goes, Sir Robert Gordon died suddenly at his breakfast table in Balmoral Castle. At the same time, Queen Victoria, Prince Albert, and their three children were enduring torrential weather in the West highlands. Heeding the royal doctor's advice that Queen Victoria would benefit from the drier and more pleasant climate of Deeside, Prince Albert quickly entered negotiations with the Fife Trustees to take over the lease of Balmoral Castle, complete with its furniture and staff.

The first visit by Queen Victoria and Prince Albert to Balmoral Castle took place in September 1848. Prince Albert decided to purchase Balmoral outright as well as the neighboring estate of Birkall and the lease of Abergeldie in the name of the Prince of Wales, the future Edward VII, who was seven years old at the time. Balmoral was thus his personal estate and did not come under the administration of the other royal residences.

Victoria and Albert's growing family, along with the administrative and social necessities of a royal household, made it clear that extending the existing Castle wouldn't suffice. In 1852 the decision was made to build a brand new castle, 100m from the site of the old one. William Smith, the City architect of Aberdeen and son of John Smith, who designed the earlier Castle, was commissioned to design a new castle that would sit around a central clock tower that would reach a height of 100 feet and would be large enough to house 130 people at a time.

Balmoral Castle has two main blocks, the 'offices' and the royal and guest apartments, both with central courtyards and linked to the tower by two-story wings. Described as a restrained version of 19th century 'Scotch Baronial' architecture, the Castle features round towers and turrets and a carriage porch entrance bearing the arms of Prince Albert in marble. Balmoral Castle is made of local

grey granite quarried from Invergelder on the estate, and the roofing slates are from Foundland in central Aberdeenshire.

Building work began in 1853; Victoria and Albert moved into the royal apartments in 1855, and by 1856 work was complete, and the old Castle was demolished. Up until his sudden death in 1861, Prince Albert had an active role in making various improvements to the estate, rebuilding cottages, creating plantations, improving the approach to Balmoral, and developing a model dairy. Following Albert's death, Queen Victoria continued to visit Balmoral and spent increasing amounts of time there until her own death in 1901. The royal family has continued to use Balmoral Castle for annual autumn visits up to the present day.

Balmoral Castle is a Historic Scotland category A listed building and is located within the Cairngorms National Park. Balmoral working estate includes a grouse moor, farmland, public fishing and hiking, and managed herds of Highland cattle, deer, and ponies. In 1931, Balmoral Castle was first opened to the public. A visit includes a tour of the largest room in the Castle, the Ballroom, and access to the gardens and exhibitions. There is no access to Balmoral during the months of August, September, and October as the Royal Family are in residence.

WHAT MAKES BALMORAL FAMOUS?

Balmoral's fame undoubtedly comes from its royal connection. Although still used by the Royal Family during the Autumn months, Balmoral will always be known as the home of Queen Victoria and Prince Albert. The monarchy's purchasing of a Scottish estate and adoption of Scottish architectural style in the mid 19th century went a long way in promoting highland culture to the rest of Scotland and solidifying the relationship between the two largest countries in Great Britain.

BALMORAL IN TV AND FILM

Balmoral Estate has been used as a location for the following films and TV shows.

- The World from Above (2010) TV Series
- Romeo and Juliet Revisited (2002) Film
- Prince William: A Royal Portrait (1999) Documentary
- The Queen Mother: A Royal Century (1999) Documentary
- Network First: Victoria and Albert (1997) TV Series
- Sixty Glorious Years (1938) Film
- Arrival of Edward II at Balmoral (1901) Documentary
- Review of the Yeoman of the Guard (1899) Documentary
- Review of the Highland Clans (1899) Documentary
- The Highland Reel (1899) Documentary
- The Highland Fling (1899) Documentary
- The Queen and Princess of Battenburg (1899) Documentary

The following films were set at Balmoral Castle, but filming was done elsewhere.

- The Queen (2006) Film
- Mrs. Brown (1997) Film

FURTHER RESEARCH

- Cuthbert Graham (1972) Portrait of Aberdeen and Deeside
- Newbury, Williams, and Jolles (1984) Balmoral Castle: Great Houses
- Rodney Castleden (2013) The Castles and Britain and Ireland
- David Cook (2000) Castles of Scotland
- Ronald Clarke (2011) Balmoral: Queen Victoria's Highland Home

VISITING INFORMATION

Balmoral Castle is open to the public from the 1st April to 31st July each year and opening hours are between 10.00 am and 5.00 pm when the Royal Family is not in residence. For more information, visit the website www.balmoralcastle.com

MEETING THE QUEEN
A USER'S GUIDE

So you have a chance to meet Her Majesty, Queen Elizabeth II, but you're not sure what to do, eh? Okay, maybe you're not that lucky, but just curious anyway. Well, have no fear because we at Anglotopia have thought long and hard about this on the off chance it should ever happen to us. Protocol is very important in any dealings with the Royal Family and while the Monarchy's website states that "there are no obligatory codes of behavior when meeting the Queen or a member of the Royal Family," you can certainly expect to make the news if you don't follow "traditional forms."

It doesn't matter whether you're an ordinary citizen or the President of the United States; there is quite a list of protocol rules to follow when meeting Queen Elizabeth. One of the first things one must do is to be early. It's normally rude to keep someone waiting, but it's especially rude to keep the Queen waiting, considering she is the single most important person in the kingdom. The next is the formation of everyone who will meet her. Sometimes visitors will be lined up for greetings, but in more intimate gatherings, semi-circles might be more prevalent.

Once the big moment arrives, the rules diverge a little for men and women. Men are expected to give a neck bow (just the head bowing at the Queen), while women are expected to curtsey. If you're not a British citizen or Commonwealth citizen, this isn't expected but is still considered polite. Typically one should wait until spoken to, and then the first address to the Queen should use "Your Majesty," while any subsequent address can use this or "Ma'am," pronounced as in "jam" as we would say in the United States.

Conversation is also strictly observed. It should be limited to "small talk," and no personal subjects should ever be addressed. If you're sitting next to her at dinner, she will always speak to the guest of honor on her right during the first course before turning to the guest on her left in the next course. Formula 1 driver Lewis Hamilton found this out the hard way when he tried to engage her in conversation, only to be told he had to wait his turn.

Touching a member of the Royal Family is a big no-no. Normally, a formal handshake is permitted, and one must wait until she extends her hand first, but anything beyond that is seen as a breach of protocol. A hug, a kiss on the cheek, or even a light touch on the shoulder is not permitted unless she initiates it, as she did with former First Lady Michelle Obama during a formal state visit, though the First Lady's hug went too far according to the British press. In 1992, former Australian PM Paul Keating got quite the media drubbing when he put his arm around Her Majesty uninvited. Giving gifts is permitted, though mostly reserved for heads of state and visiting dignitaries.

Lastly, one should never do anything before the Queen. It's customary to wait to sit until she does, and one should not begin eating until she begins the meal. Conversely, when she finishes the meal, you should be finished too. However, the dinner portion of a formal state visit can take quite a while, especially when table conversations are involved, so it's not been an issue in years. Most importantly, unless you have a special permission to do so by the private secretary, you should not leave before the Queen does. When you do leave, you should avoid turning your back to her.

And now you have a basic guide to meeting Queen Elizabeth II. With some differences, roughly the same rules apply to meeting any other member of the Royal Family, so you'll be fairly prepared for the Duke and Duchess of Cambridge, the Duke and Duchess of Sussex, Prince Andrew, Prince Charles, and more. More can be found on the Monarch's website and other sites online, so if you have more specific questions, there are plenty of sources available to help you.

This article was excerpted from 101 UK Culture Tips: A Field Guide to British Culture available from booksellers everywhere.

THE CONCEPT OF THE CROWN

The Crown in the UK is both a concept and an object. The object sits on the head of the reigning Monarch. The Crown of State is kept in the Tower of London when not in use (the Queen only wears it on special occasions).

The Crown as a concept is more complicated.

The Crown, in the simplest terms, is the State of the United Kingdom and everything in it.

In legal terms, a type of corporation, the Crown is the legal embodiment of executive, legislative, and judicial governance in the monarchy of the United Kingdom. The concept of the Crown developed first in England as a separation of the literal Crown and property of the kingdom from the person and personal property of the Monarch. It spread through English and later British colonization and is now rooted in the legal lexicon of the United Kingdom, its Crown dependencies, and the other 15 independent realms.

The term is also found in various expressions such as "Crown land," which some countries refer to as "public land" or "state land,"; as well as in some offices, such as minister of the Crown, Crown attorney, and Crown prosecutor.

The Crown is immortal. It never dies. It is eternal. Even if the current Monarch dies, the Crown immediately passes to the next heir, in an uninterrupted line. The Crown can never cease. The reigning Monarch is the living embodiment of the concept of the Crown and the personification of the State.

The concept of the Crown took form under early feudal systems in the British Isles. Though not used this way in all countries that had this system, in England, all rights and privileges were ultimately bestowed by the ruler. Land, for instance, was granted by the Crown to lords in exchange for feudal services, and they, in turn, granted the land to lesser lords.

The body of the reigning sovereign holds two distinct personas in constant coexistence: that of a natural-born human being and that of the British State as accorded to him or her through law; the Crown and the Monarch are conceptually divisible but legally indivisible, the office cannot exist without the officeholder.

The reigning king or Queen is the employer of all government officials and staff (including the viceroys, judges, members of the armed forces, police officers, and parliamentarians), the guardian of foster children (Crown wards), as well as the owner of all state lands (Crown land), buildings and equipment (Crown-held property), state-owned companies (Crown corporations), and the copyright for government publications (Crown copyright). This is all in his or her position as sovereign, not as an individual; all such property is held by the Crown in perpetuity and cannot be sold by the sovereign without the proper advice and consent of his or her relevant ministers.

The Crown also represents the legal embodiment of executive, legislative, and judicial governance. While the Crown's legal personality is usually regarded as a corporation sole, it can, at least for some purposes, be described as a corporation aggregate headed by the Monarch.

For example, the Queen does not need to carry a passport or get a driving license because they are all issued in her name. She is above the State, above the citizenry. It's a bit bizarre. To make it even more confusing, HM The Queen has her own property portfolio and collections that she owns personally and is not part of the Crown Estate.

The Crown Estate is a collection of lands and holdings in the territories of England, Wales, and Northern Ireland within the United Kingdom belonging to the British Monarch as a corporation sole, making it "the sovereign's public estate," which is neither government property nor part of the Monarch's private estate. It cannot be sold or divided by the Monarch. Now, the Crown Estate used to be under the control of the Monarch, but this was given up several hundred years ago when a monarch was deep in debt. In exchange for a yearly subsidy to run the Royal household and affairs, control of the estate was given to the British government. However, the Monarch still has possessions in their personal capacity that are not part of the Crown Estate.

As I said, it's very confusing but endlessly fascinating.

This article was excerpted from 101 UK Culture Tips: A Field Guide to British Culture available from booksellers everywhere.

HOUSES FIT FOR A QUEEN
A GUIDE TO THE ROYAL ESTATES

It's hard to keep track of how many homes the Queen has. Big and small(-ish), they are dotted all over the United Kingdom. Some are privately owned by the monarch's personal holdings, like Sandringham and Balmoral, but many are state-owned, like Buckingham, Windsor, and Kensington Palace. Some we hear a lot about, like the granddaddy of them all, Buckingham Palace, some are much lesser-known, like Hillsborough Castle, the Queen's royal residence in Northern Ireland. Some are royal palaces while no longer being royal residences—Hampton Court Palace, the Palace of Westminster, and the Tower of London (one wonders if that was ever a very comfortable residence). Besides Buckingham Palace, her daily residence and office, she never stays very long in one home, yet she likes to come back to it as though she's just walked out the door. One of her staff at her estate in Norfolk says, "If bits and knickknacks were left on chairs, they are kept on chairs." There are too many royal homes to discuss each one separately, but let's take a closer look at a few.

Buckingham Palace

Buckingham Palace is the official London residence of the Queen and the offices of the Monarchy and the home that most people easily associate with the Queen. When Elizabeth is not traveling, this is her weekday residence with 775 rooms and about 40 acres of gardens, surrounded by numerous royal public parks (Hyde Park, Green Park, St. James's Park) with the Queen Victoria Memorial front and center outside the gates. It is also where she delivered two of her children, Charles and Andrew.

Originally known as Buckingham House and the home of the Duke of Buckingham, the oldest part of the Palace, the wine vaults, dates back to 1760. It was first acquired by King George III and, at one point, was considered as a permanent home for the British Library; it was not used as a royal residence until Queen Victoria moved in. She greatly expanded and renovated the Palace—she had a lot of kids, staff, and parties. There are rumors of underground passageways linking the Palace with Whitehall, Parliament, and Clarence House, but no one can quite get confirmation of their existence.

The balcony, which is now the favorite photo spot of the Royal Family, was first used by Queen Victoria to give the royal wave, opening the Great Exhibition in 1951. King George IV started the tradition of ending the Trooping of the Colour, the monarch's birthday celebration, from the balcony.

During World War II, Buckingham Palace was hit by the Luftwaffe nine times. The second bomb destroyed the Palace Chapel in 1940 and almost killed the King and Queen (George VI and Elizabeth, Queen Elizabeth's parents). Queen Elizabeth, the Queen Mother, said, "I'm glad we've been bombed. It makes me feel I can look the East End in the face." Today the Palace has a helicopter pad outside (as we remember from the opening of the London Olympics when James Bond comes to fetch Queen Elizabeth from the Palace) and a houseful of dogs inside. Parts of the house are open to the public in the summer months when the Royal Family is their estate in Scotland, a clever solution to raise funds to pay for the cost of rebuilding Windsor Castle after the fire that nearly destroyed it in 1992. Queen Elizabeth II can be seen in the halls with her tell-tale purse over her arm. When asked why she carries it in the house, her response was, "This house is very big, you know."

Windsor Castle

Windsor is the largest inhabited castle in the world as well as the longest inhabited and is the weekend home of the royal family. Elizabeth and her children consider Windsor their real home. Elizabeth says "all the happiest memories of childhood" were at Windsor, and when her two younger children were growing up, they spent a lot of time riding their scooters in the halls and playing hide and seek on the grounds. The family spends a month here at Easter as well as a week in June for Royal Ascot and Garter Day. During World War II, Margaret and Elizabeth lived at Windsor to stay away from the Luftwaffe bombs—it was equipped with a bomb shelter and anti-aircraft guns on the roof.

The Castle was first built by William the Conqueror as a defense on the outskirts of London, just a day's ride from the Tower of London. It was later rebuilt by Henry II, Edward III, Charles II after the Restoration, and George IV, but the

greatest modern rebuilding was after the fire in 1992 when a large portion of the Castle was destroyed (we'll discuss that further in another article). With such a long history, it might not be a surprise to know that many of the staff and family consider the Castle to be haunted; Queen Elizabeth II says she's seen the first Queen Elizabeth's ghost here.

As the Queen's favorite home, she takes great care with it and her guests. She hosts foreign heads of state who arrive by horse-drawn carriage, as well as friends and family. When these guests come, she inspects their bedrooms and chooses books to leave on their nightstands. She knows all about the paintings on the walls, telling her guests about the Holbeins and the Rubens they're looking at. Elizabeth has always done a lot of horseback riding on the grounds, as well, although refusing to wear a helmet: "The only thing that comes between the Queen and her heir is a Hermes scarf."

St. George's Chapel at Windsor has seen royal weddings, including the current Prince Edward's, and is open to the public for daily services (the Queen believes that everyone should benefit from the royal estates). The Chapel was also the site of Princess Margaret's funeral and the burial site of ten British monarchs, including Henry VIII and the Queen's parents George VI and Elizabeth.

Queen Victoria first opened the state apartments to the public in 1845, also believing that everyone should benefit from the royal estates. The Royal Archives, Print Room, and the Royal Library are housed at Windsor Castle now. A visit to the Castle and its grounds is a great day trip from London for many tourists today.

Balmoral

Balmoral is one of the Queen's Scottish residences, located in the Highlands a few hours north of Edinburgh. Prince Philip oversees all the royal estates, yet despite it being located on 50,000 acres and comprising numerous houses on the property, the estate manager says, "Her Majesty is aware of everything" that goes on there, she knows the property inside and out, spending hours walking, riding, and driving (herself) around the grounds. On one such walk, she ran into a local who commented that she looked an awful lot like

the Queen. Her response: "How reassuring."

The Queen and her family spend the months of August and September at Balmoral every year, resting, exploring, hosting the Prime Minister and his family for a weekend, and throwing picnics and barbeques where Philip grills and Elizabeth makes the tea and does the washing up (a sight that many find disconcerting). The Queen says of her long visits, "It's nice to hibernate for a bit when one leads such a very moveable life," and "To be able to sleep in the same bed for six weeks is a nice change." Not much has changed at Balmoral since Queen Victoria bought the property. It is still privately owned by the monarch, with Queen Victoria's dogs buried alongside Queen Elizabeth II's in the pet cemetery on the property. Elizabeth commented that "there is a certain fascination in keeping the place as Queen Victoria had it."

Elizabeth holds many fond memories of Balmoral—it's where Philip proposed to her, it's where she shot her first stag with her father and caught her first salmon; she can act like a local visiting shops (although shopkeepers have noticed that she sometimes has a hard time sorting out the money in her wallet), and she does chores like pulling weeds, particularly when she's frustrated about something. It was also where she had her first training in wartime service when her father, King George VI, opened a house on the estate as a refuge for mothers and children evacuated from Glasgow during World War II. Today visitors can run a 5K on the grounds, take a safari in a jeep, stay in some of the cottages as rental properties, and play golf.

Palace of Holyroodhouse

Holyroodhouse is located at the end of the Royal Mile in Edinburgh, like bookends with Edinburgh Castle on the other end. It is the official Scottish residence of the monarch and has a long and fascinating history. The house began as an Augustinian monastery with David I in 1128 and was renovated into a palace, not much of which still stands today, by James IV and Margaret Tudor in 1501. Mary Queen of Scots spent most of her Scottish reign here; it's where she married both husbands and where her favored secretary, David Rizzio, was brutally stabbed by her husband Lord

Darnley and his cohorts while she and her pregnant belly (the future James VI of Scotland and I of England) were held at knifepoint in the adjoining room.

King George V and Queen Mary, Queen Elizabeth II's grandparents, started the tradition of the yearly Garden Party at Holyroodhouse. They also renovated the Palace with electricity, bathrooms, and elevators. Elizabeth and Philip have continued the Garden Parties, hosting about 8000 guests every year during Holyrood Week. If you're lucky enough to be in town for Holyrood Week like we were a few years ago, you see hundreds of finely dressed royals and commoners walking the Royal Mile in their fancy hats on the way to the Garden Party, and if you climb Arthur's Seat just above the Palace, you get a great view of the whole party in the back garden. It does, however, mean you don't get to visit the inside of the Palace as it's closed to tours the whole week.

Sandringham House

Sandringham House is the Queen's privately-owned country escape in Norfolk and has been a home of British monarchs since 1862. King George V called it "Dear Old Sandringham." Since the time of Queen Victoria, the royal family has spent Christmas at the estate (except during World War II when it was too dangerous to travel). It is from here that the Queen gives her yearly Christmas address.

In 1870, the future King Edward VII, son of Queen Victoria, built a new and improved house on the Sandringham estate with over 300 elaborate and ornate rooms, red brick and stone, balconies and bay windows, and supposedly, ghosts. One guest was surprised to see in her bedroom three sinks. One for "Head & Face Only," one for "Hands," and of the last, she said, "Good heavens, the last was blank, so what can it have been for?" The kennels on the estate were established by King Edward VII in 1879 and are still a favorite of Queen Elizabeth. Here she helps name her puppies as well as burying some of her beloved dogs. The thousands of acres of gardens and park are open to the public for free, with public roads crisscrossing the property.

Kensington Palace

Kensington Palace was home to monarchs until 1760, with King George II the last monarch in residence. It is where Queen Victoria was born, where she learned of her accession to the throne, and where she first met Prince Albert. Kensington became a royal palace when William and Mary bought the house in 1689 and commissioned the great Christopher Wren to renovate and rebuild it. Located at the end of Kensington Gardens, one can walk through from the Palace through Kensington Gardens, Hyde Park, and Green Park and reach Buckingham Palace at the other end. It is now the home of the Duke and Duchess of Cambridge, William and Catherine, and their children, as well as Prince Harry, and formerly Princess Diana and Princess Margaret. Queen Victoria opened the King and Queen's State Apartments to the public in 1898, and parts of it are still open today to visitors. Visitors can see the impressive Royal Ceremonial Dress Collection and have tea in one of the greatest tearooms in London, the Orangery.

The Royal Yacht Brittania

While not technically a royal estate, the Brittania was launched in 1953, the year of Elizabeth's coronation, and was helped in its design by Prince Philip, an officer of the Royal Navy. The royal family considered it their home away from home (whatever home that was). They spent many happy vacations and royal tours on the yacht; it was somewhere the public couldn't reach them. They played games on the deck, toured the Western Isles of the United Kingdom, and took honeymoons on board. One foreign secretary commented, "There was a magic about the Brittania which had nothing to do with magnificence because she wasn't a magnificent ship. . . . She was homely in the proper sense." And Princess Anne said of the yacht, "We found as children that there was so much to do, we expended so much energy that we couldn't describe our time on the yacht as a rest." And the children didn't rest on board. They were given chores like cleaning the lifeboats and helping with the cooking. While onboard, each child was given a member of staff as "Sea Daddy" to keep an eye on them and help them stay entertained or on task.

In 1994, Prime Minister John Major announced that the cost was too great and the Brittania would be retired. The family took their last tour of the Scottish isles in 1997 and retired the ship. It now docks in Edinburgh and is open for visits where you can take a self-guided tour of the elaborate staterooms, galley, and bridge, stopping for lunch in the elegant (though crowded) tearoom. The decommissioning ceremony was one of the only times the public has ever seen Queen Elizabeth shed a tear.

In an average year, the royal family hosts over 50,000 guests at Buckingham Palace and 8000 guests at Holyroodhouse. The Queen has strict rules about wearing hats only before 6:00 pm, no touching, and how to address the royalty. She has a code with her staff of how she holds her purse—placed on the table is a five-minute warning, on the floor means "I'm ready to get out of here," left arm means "all is well." The family has a signal to get overstaying guests out of the house, asking the footman if the car is ready. The staff knows not to move things and that the Queen likes all the horse races recorded, that her horse trainers are always connected directly to her private line, and that nobody sits in Queen Victoria's chair. The list of intricacies goes on and on. With so many houses and so many staff to maintain them, it's a surprisingly well-oiled machine.

MODERNIZING THE MONARCHY
How The Crown Has Changed With Britain

Depending on how you count, Britain has seen sixty-six monarchs since the Anglo-Saxon King Egbert in 827; Elizabeth II is the fortieth monarch to reign since William the Conqueror in 1066. Elizabeth has been on the throne since 1952, a whopping 66 years, making her only one of five British monarchs to rule longer than fifty years and the only to rule for 70 years (she has broken Victoria's record!).

In 1957, in her first televised Christmas message, Elizabeth spoke of herself bringing in a "new Elizabethan age" reminiscent of her namesake and the Elizabethan renaissance of the arts and economic prosperity and power. She did, however, draw the line at comparing herself to the previous Elizabeth's character, saying in a broadcast in 1953, "frankly I do not myself feel at all like my great Tudor forebear, who was blessed with neither husband nor children, who ruled as a despot and was never able to leave her native shores." Our Queen Elizabeth had a husband and four children and has traveled more than any other world leader, visiting more than 115 countries. She has brought the British monarchy into the modern age with her acceptance of technology, her willingness to listen to and learn from criticism, and her progressive views towards her beloved Commonwealth.

The late Prince Philip can be thanked for a lot of the advances in technology that Elizabeth has embraced during her reign. It was Philip's idea to televise the coronation in 1953, a notion that Elizabeth didn't jump on from the start but was willing to accept (except for a few concessions about close-ups and her anointing). Prince Philip acted as Chancellor of Cambridge University as well as Edinburgh University; he encouraged technology and innovation and was a great conservationist. It was at Philip's encouragement that the Queen switched her Christmas broadcast from radio to television in 1957 and helped her to use the Teleprompter. The switch to a televised broadcast was a huge success. 1958 saw the first televised broadcast of the Queen opening Parliament; it proved to be a great reminder that as sovereign, she has a place in the government beside her Prime Minister.

Philip found a like-minded confidant and cohort in his uncle, Dickie Mountbatten, although Mountbatten might have been considered a little too progressive by the general public. It was with Uncle Dickie's help that Philip in 1969 convinced the Queen to allow a documentary to be made of the royal family, trying to make them more real, more 3-dimensional. Their daughter Anne always thought it was "a rotten idea," and David Attenborough (of Planet Earth fame), a friend of Philip's and a BBC broadcaster at the time, said it was a dangerous idea, that "the monarchy depends on the mystique." It was, of course, hugely popular, shown repeatedly on television until the family decided that was enough and it was time to replace the veil of secrecy (it has never been repeated by the BBC, but copies can be found).

Elizabeth and the Palace faced a new kind of scrutiny with Lord Altrincham in 1957. Altrincham was a writer, politician, Baron (even though he eventually gave up his title), and somewhat surprisingly, a monarchist. He criticized the Queen as being stiff and out of touch with her people, yet he meant it as a way to strengthen the monarchy— he wanted the Palace to listen and make positive changes. It was in his article in August of 1957 that he suggested the Queen televise her Christmas broadcast, an idea that Philip promoted and convinced the Queen to put into practice.

Besides just televising the address, he wanted to Queen to loosen up in all her speeches: "The Queen's speech, I feel, her own natural self is not allowed to come through. It's a sort of synthetic creature that speaks. Not the Queen as she really is. If she herself were allowed to speak, the effect would be wonderful." And the effect was wonderful; the viewing public got to see a glimpse of the real person, something she's tried to give (in small doses) ever since. A suggestion that Altrincham made public but that the Palace was already considering was doing away with presenting debutantes to the Queen at the Debutante Ball. With that suggestion, a Palace official noted that they actually held off on that one, not wanting to seem that they were doing everything Altrincham asked of them. Lord Altrincham received his own criticism for his criticism, with the Archbishop of Canterbury hurling such heavy insults as calling him "a very silly man" and a loyal supporter of the Queen striking him on the street after giving a television interview. Yet the royal family took his ideas seriously enough to implement them, even bringing in David Attenborough to coach the Queen on her public speaking. She and Philip

were soon inviting a wider range of the public to events at Buckingham Palace and the Garden Party at Holyroodhouse in Edinburgh, as well as trying to reach out and seem more real to the country. Altrincham met with Elizabeth's secretary and great supporter, Martin Charteris, who later said of Altrincham's suggestions: "You did a great service to the monarchy, and I'm glad to say so publicly."

Queen Elizabeth II has spent about half of her reign traveling around the Commonwealth while the definition of the Commonwealth has changed. "It is easy enough to define what the Commonwealth is not. Indeed this is quite a popular pastime," she once said. In 1949, while her father was still King, the London Declaration took the word "Britain" out of the Commonwealth title, making King George VI at the time "Head of the Commonwealth." Former British colonies, from the days of Britain as an Empire, claimed their independence from the Crown then choose to join the Commonwealth, as India did in 1949. Or, as in the case of the Republic of Ireland, choose not to. With the end of the Empire, the designation of Commonwealth began with eight members—India, Ceylon, New Zealand, Australia, Canada, South Africa, Pakistan, and of course, Britain.

By the 21st century, the Commonwealth had 54 member countries, about a third of the world's population. Of this change and growth in the Commonwealth, the Queen has said, "The transformation of the Crown from an emblem of dominion into a symbol of free and voluntary association ... Has no precedent." The Commonwealth acts as a system to promote good government, civil rights, education, and economic development; the Queen takes her role as Head of the Commonwealth very seriously, even denying entry into the Commonwealth for countries that fail to adhere to the fair governing standards expected of them (for example, Rhodesia when they wanted to establish an oppressive white-minority government). Head of the Commonwealth is, in fact, a different title than her title as Her Majesty the Queen--it is not a hereditary title but an appointed one that traditionally goes with the monarch but does not have to, but it is a title that she takes very seriously, treating her Commonwealth with great care and affection.

At home, the Queen also has some help promoting the values of the Commonwealth nations. Tony Blair, Elizabeth's tenth Prime Minister, was very good at helping the Queen be progressive in her reign in the United Kingdom. At his request, she opened the Scottish Parliament and visited the National Assembly for Wales, both in an attempt to gain Scotland and Wales some more of their own governing power. In her words, "I can readily understand their aspirations, but I cannot forget that I was crowned Queen of the United Kingdom of Great Britain and Northern Ireland. Perhaps this Jubilee is a time to remind ourselves of the benefits which union has conferred, at home and in our international dealings, on the inhabitants of all parts of this United Kingdom."

She showed little fear in visiting Northern Ireland during the unrest there, even against the recommendations of her advisors, commenting that violent riots or not, the people of Northern Ireland were still her countrymen. This attitude would prove even more modern and inclusive after the IRA bombing of Dickie Mountbatten's yacht off the coast of Ireland, killing Dickie and several members of the family, including two teenagers. While much of the royal family said they would never set foot in Ireland again, the Queen was forgiving (though heartbroken), recognizing that as a modern monarch, she could not appear vengeful towards part of the United Kingdom.

Even out of the Commonwealth countries—in what was once the colonies—Elizabeth proved to be embracing the modern times. She was the first British monarch to address both houses of Congress, even flying home on the newfangled Concorde. She even commented on the lessons learned from losing the colonies, speaking at a commemoration ceremony of the Liberty Bell in 1976: We have "sincere gratitude to the Founding Fathers for having taught Britain a very valuable lesson. We lost the American colonies because we lacked that statesmanship 'to know the right time and the manner of yielding what is impossible to keep.'. . . We learned to respect the right of others to govern themselves in their own ways. . . . Without that great act in the cause of liberty, we could never have transformed an empire into a commonwealth." What a wonderful lesson for her to have taken away from her predecessors' mistakes, bringing her Commonwealth into the new age.

Closer to home, in fact in the Queen's residences, Elizabeth has taken opportunities to

modernize. In 1982 when President Reagan and the First Lady were planning a trip to Windsor, the Queen and her staff heard that the couple liked showers instead of baths (not a very common fixture in the older houses and even hotels these days in Britain). The first shower was installed at Windsor Castle ahead of the American visit. Reagan was then the first American President to speak to both houses of Parliament, praising the country's response in the Falkland Islands.

The Lord Chamberlain, David Airlie, who was in charge of Palace operations in the 1980s, decided to make some changes, as well. He commissioned a 1300 page report with 188 recommendations to streamline workings at the Palace offices and residence (he must have thought Buckingham was still reminiscent of Prince Albert's days of frustration when one footman carried the firelogs but was not allowed to light the fire, that was someone else's job). In 1990, Airlie also updated the Civil List, giving the Queen more access to her own money. The Civil List is or was from 1760 until then, a complicated and convoluted method of managing the royal family's money. It was reviewed every ten years with no shortage of angst on everyone's parts.

In short, the Civil List was basically the Queen's allowance from the government, yet she put that money into the fund from her own portfolio of investments and property (so really, it was Parliament portioning out her own money

back to her). It seemed to always be a source of concern and confusion, and while Airlie's update of the Civil List helped simplify and alleviate the bad press, by 2013, it was scrapped altogether and replaced with the Sovereign Grant. This new plan allowed the Crown to get their own funds out of the Crown Estates Portfolio—using their own money to support their own needs, giving the Palace more control over their spending minimizing government involvement. The Queen also agreed to pay taxes, which was a huge concession on her part, earning a lot of public support and revenue for the government.

Perhaps one of the greatest examples of her willingness to adapt is just recently with the opening ceremonies of the London Olympics in 2012 when the Queen herself appeared in a video clip with Daniel Craig as James Bond (talk about popular appeal). She texts her grandchildren, sends emails, pays taxes, yet maintains her same standards, promoting the same message throughout her long reign as she did in a Christmas broadcast in 1975: "It does matter what each individual does each day ... Kindness, sympathy, resolution and courteous behavior are infectious." From the Queen's early days as a mechanic in World War II to driving the very stunned Crown Prince Abdullah of Saudi Arabia around Balmoral herself, Elizabeth has always been rather progressive. As one of the few female heads of state, she would have to be fearless and unafraid to embrace the changing world.

THE QUEEN'S ANNUS HORRIBILIS

1992 - THE TERRIBLE YEAR FOR THE MONARCHY

1992 was not the Queen's best year; it was so bad it had to be expressed in Latin. In fact, she says herself, "Nineteen ninety-two is not a year on which I shall look back with undiluted pleasure. In the words of one of my more sympathetic correspondents, it has turned out to be an 'Annus Horribilis.' " The year looked promising enough, it was the celebration of her fortieth year on the throne, and her forty-fifth wedding anniversary, she had just had her third State visit to the United States and flown on the Concorde, she was the first British monarch to address both houses of the U.S. Congress. In February, her sanctioned BBC documentary E II R aired on television to great success. That was the end of the celebrations for her accession. In March, Prince Andrew and Fergie separate with loads of press coverage; in April, Princess Anne gets a divorce only to re-marry in later in the year; the summer is filled with scandals around Princess Diana; November sees the biggest blow of all, a huge blaze at Windsor Castle.

Prince Andrew and his wife had been in a rocky relationship for a while, but in January of 1992, the Daily Mail published photos of Fergie and Steve Wyatt, a Texas oil tycoon, on vacation together with young Princess Beatrice in the South of France. The photos leave little to the imagination; a couple of months later, they're followed by the announcement that the Duke and Duchess of York are splitting up. Several months after that, Fergie is in the news again with pictures of her "financial adviser" John Bryan sucking on her toes, again in France. In the BBC documentary shown earlier in the year, the Queen is quoted saying, "Most people have a job, and then they go home, and in this existence, the job and the life go on together, because you can't really divide it up. I think this is what the younger members find difficult, the regimented side of it." She was not speaking of Andrew and Fergie's marital trouble in particular, but the message is the same--the strict royal life is not for everyone. While Fergie's mess in the press hurt the royal family, it was nothing compared to what was on the way with Diana.

The year previous, Prince Charles's wife, Diana the Princess of Wales, had collaborated with Andrew Morton on a tell-all biography, Diana: Her True Story. While Diana consistently denied any involvement in the book, it soon became clear that she had deceived the royal family and the Palace. Excerpts of the book started coming out at the beginning of 1992, the contents making it clear that she had participated in the book. In it, she talks of being "trapped in a loveless marriage" and of her struggles with bulimia and suicide. She plays up her loneliness for the press, making sad faces in front of the Taj Mahal and generally putting herself forth as the victim of the Crown's machinations, all while sharing far too many private details for anyone's comfort.

In the summer comes "Squidgygate," newly-released recordings of private phone calls between Diana and her "friend" James Gilbey. It's a toss-up which was worse, the recordings or the book, but they were both fuel for the media fire. The Sun released the tapes from a telephone conversation on New Year's Eve while Diana was at Sandringham celebrating Christmas with Charles and the royal family. In it, Gilbey calls Diana "Squidgy," they profess their love repeatedly amidst endearments, innuendo, and profanities, with slurs against Charles and the whole family. She tells him, "my life is torture."

The royal family is clearly bothered by what she's said and by her lack of discretion. The royal family loves their discretion and loyalty, and lately, Diana has been a string of disloyalties. The Palace is bothered by how the recordings came about—nobody's supposed to listen in on their Royal Highnesses. The recordings came from a ham radio operator, but after a formal inquiry, it seemed that a regular ham operator shouldn't have been able to access a royal phone like that, so the question remained, where did they come from? The biggest rumor was that it was British intelligence, a plausible explanation considering the threat the royal family was under from the IRA. Other rumors were, of course, that Diana leaked them herself. Whatever the source, Diana was getting huge press and seemed to be loving it while the Palace and the Queen hated every minute of it. Diana thought the royal family was just jealous of her good press, but her whole

attitude was more vengeful than that. The Queen, Prince Philip, and Charles were made out as the bad guys. Even Princess Margaret, who had been the closest to Diana in the family, had enough of the nonsense and threw all her loyalty in with her sister and family.

Throughout the experience, the Queen maintained a civil attitude and even showed kindness towards Diana, something she didn't get a lot of credit for. While Fergie's media circus was bad, she was never mean-spirited, always seeming fun-loving and careless, while Diana's media affair quickly seemed more calculated and devious. Prime Minister John Major finally announced Diana and Charles's divorce in November.

November 20th was Philip and Elizabeth's 45th wedding anniversary. Prince Philip was spending it on royal duties in Argentina; Elizabeth spent it watching her beloved Windsor Castle go up in flames. With over a thousand rooms, it had survived William the Conqueror, two World Wars, and threats from the IRA (who were initially suspected of starting the blaze). The fire started with some wiring during renovation work, the curtains caught first, and the fire spread quickly through all the wood, fabric, and high ceilings in the Castle. Prince Andrew was at the Castle when it happened and called his mother in London to rush out to Windsor.

We see pictures of her in rubber boots, surrounded by police, firemen, the Household Cavalry, family, the Dean of Windsor, and crowds of townspeople all forming human chains to pull valuable artwork and heirlooms to the safety of moving trucks and army convoys. At one point, the Queen went into the Castle to direct the removal of the valuables. People remember seeing Holbeins and Rembrandts leaning against vans in the parking lot to get them safely out of the way. Because of the renovations in part of the house that caught fire first, much of the artwork had already been removed, just in case. And the private apartments were immediately sealed off to protect them from the blaze. But still, it took 250 firemen about fifteen hours to stop the fire, by which point it had damaged 100 rooms, including the Queen's Private Chapel dating from the 13th century. A spokesman for the Royal

Institute of Architects said, "It's a heartbreaking loss. The chapel was beautiful, and the works of art inside are quite irreplaceable."

The blaze spread quickly; firefighters commented that it climbed the staircases faster than they could and was difficult to battle. The high ceilings and towers meant it was challenging to get the blast of the fire hose to the right places and that there were no sprinklers installed, and as it was built as a Norman castle by William the Conqueror, one side faced a steep drop off (castle defenses at work), meaning the firefighters couldn't even get around one side of the building. By the time all the assessments were made, the cost of damages reached at least 50 million pounds. Originally Parliament said it would cover the cost of repairs, which seemed only fair since they also legislated that royal residences cannot be insured. But after a public outcry over tax dollars being used to repair the Queen's house, the Queen and Palace officials had to come up with another plan. The solution was to raise money by opening Buckingham Palace for public tours during the summer when the royal family was away at Balmoral. The Queen also began paying taxes herself, something that was already in the works anyway but was just pushed ahead quicker to alleviate all the bad press Queen Elizabeth and her family were facing.

Elizabeth considered Windsor her childhood home; Andrew described her as "absolutely devastated," and the photos in the press clearly showed that. When the Palace Press Officer was asked what Her Majesty's reaction was, he responded very realistically, "Probably the same reaction as yours if you saw your home burning down." It was the end to a very hard year for the Queen, and she handled it the same way many of us would—evaluating the mess then going to stay with her mother.

The speech when she called the past year "Annus Horribilis" was given at the Guildhall in London and was meant to be a thank you to the nation for the support she has felt in her last forty years on the throne. It turned into something else entirely. John Major, the Prime Minister at the time, even changed his international travel plans, missing important

THE FUTURE
John Grigg looks to
the next coronation
Page 18

Were
really to bla
Page 5

THE TIMES
45p

THURSDAY DECEMBER 10 1992

No. 64,512

Queen
Mother
will go to
Scotland
By ALAN HAMILTON

Separation but no divorce for Prince and Princess

■ The separation of the Prince and Princess of Wales, announced to a hushed Commons by the prime minister, raises the prospect of a king without a queen

By ALAN HAMILTON AND NICHOLAS WOOD

meetings with Heads of State to show his continued support for the Queen. Elizabeth spoke to the crowd quietly, suffering from a bad cold most likely caught standing outside in the smoke, cold and wet all night at Windsor. "There can be no doubt, of course, that criticism is good for people and institutions that are part of public life.

No institution — City, monarchy, whatever — should expect to be free from the scrutiny of those who give it their loyalty and support, not to mention those who don't. But we are all part of the same fabric of our nation society, and scrutiny by one part of another can be just as effective if it is made with a touch of gentleness, good humor, and understanding. This sort of questioning can also act, and it should do so, as an effective engine for change." Instead of a thank you for her years on the throne, she is asking for some kindness and compassion towards her family while telling the public to be patient because their criticisms are heard and will be answered. She also has the diplomacy and foresight to comment that while the press and the public have been hard on her

family this year (not to mention physical disasters like the fire), time will temper the criticism and when they all look back on 1992, they might not think it was quite so bad after all.

After the Guildhall speech, the bad news was not over. Before the year was out, Prince Charles and Princess Diana announced they were separating. It was the first step on the road to the first modern Royal Divorce and eventually the death of Princess Diana in a tragic car accident in 1997, an event that remade the Monarchy in unexpected ways.

Even well into the 21st-century, her children - and some grandchildren - have still managed to find creative, lurid, and disappointing ways to make the Royal Family look bad. The headlines constantly read that the Monarchy is in peril, that it must change and that the Royal Family is scandal-ridden. Not much really changes there, does it!

A CHANGED BRITAIN

BRITISH HISTORY DURING THE LIFE OF ELIZABETH II

1936 – KING GEORGE V DIES AND KING EDWARD VIII ASCENDS THE THRONE

At the time of King George V's death, his son, Prince Edward, was Prince of Wales and the natural heir to the throne. As such, he ascended the throne on his father's death on January 20, 1936, but this is not where the story ends. Prior to this event, Edward had met and fallen in love with Wallis Simpson, an American divorcee. While never popular with King George V and Queen Mary nor with the British government, Edward continued to see Wallis and included her in more and more official functions as his guest. It wasn't until rumors circulated of his intention to marry her that the real trouble began.

1936 – KING EDWARD VIII ABDICATES AND KING GEORGE VI ASCENDS THE THRONE

As the Monarch is the head of the Church of England, it was not constitutionally permitted for King Edward to marry a woman who was divorced with still-living ex-husbands. Facing resistance from the British Government as well as the Church of England, Edward was faced with the choice of breaking off his relationship with Wallis or abdicating the throne. On December 10, 1936, Edward officially signed his abdication notices, and his brother became King George VI. King George would subsequently lead the United Kingdom through World War II and partly through the 1950s before passing away of lung cancer. Edward and Wallis would marry and remain together for the rest of their lives.

1941 – THE BLITZ

Perhaps the greatest test of Britain's resolve against Nazi Germany, the Blitz, began in September 1940 after Germany lost air superiority during daytime hours in the Battle of Britain. While many of Britain's cities that were important to the war effort were attacked, London bore the worst of it, being hit 56 times over the course of 57 nights. As British morale remained high in the face of the bombing, the Nazis opted to move their resources to the planned invasion of Russia in the summer of 1941.

1947 – INDIA GAINS INDEPENDENCE

After the Indian Independence movement had been in existence for ninety years, the United Kingdom under Attlee finally returned self-governance through the Indian Independence Act 1947. Based on the Mountbatten Plan by Lord Mountbatten, it also resulted in the Partition of India and Pakistan. The Partition had far-reaching repercussions both for relations between India and Pakistan as well as the future demographics of the United Kingdom.

1948 – POST-WAR IMMIGRATION BEGINS

After the Partition, Indian and Pakistani residents began immigrating to the United Kingdom in large numbers to find work and escape the violence that resulted from the split. In 1948, they were joined by the Windrush Generation, who were brought from the Caribbean with the promise of permanent residency in the United Kingdom for persons from Commonwealth nations. The immigrants who came to Britain on this promise helped to diversify and enrich Britain's culture in the ensuing decades.

1948 – NATIONAL HEALTH SERVICE FOUNDED

While Parliament passed the National Health Service Act in 1946, it would be another two years before the NHS was formally established. The NHS established universal healthcare for the United Kingdom, with the NHS divided into four organizations for each member country of the UK. In the years since its creation, millions of Britons have received a majority of their medical care for free. While it has not always been without its issues, the NHS has undoubtedly been a benefit to British society.

1951 – FESTIVAL OF BRITAIN

A centennial celebration of the Great Exhibition of 1851, the Festival of Britain offered a look at recovery and Britain's future after World War II. From new developments in cinema to the advent of international modernist architecture in the UK, the festival gave hope in a time when it was most

needed. One of the buildings constructed for the Festival of Britain, the Royal Festival Hall, is still standing.

1952 – KING GEORGE VI DIES, QUEEN ELIZABETH II'S REIGN BEGINS

It was truly the end of an era when King George VI died in 1952. He had presided over the constitutional crisis that put him on the throne and guided the country through the dark days of WWII. His daughter then became Queen Elizabeth II, the longest-reigning Monarch in the country's history and one of its most transformative figures.

1953 – DISCOVERY OF DNA STRUCTURE

Undeniably one of the most important scientific discoveries of the 20th Century, American biologist James Watson and English physicist Francis Crick cracked open the mystery of DNA in 1953. The two Cambridge scientists were able to discover the structure of DNA and how it served as the building blocks for all life.

1955 – FIRST COMMERCIAL TELEVISION BROADCAST FROM ITV

The Television Act 1954 allowed for non-state-owned television networks to form, the first of which was Independent Television, or ITV, in 1955. The network began with six franchises spread across Britain and has been responsible for some of British television's best-known programs, such as The Adventures of Sherlock Holmes, The Avengers, Foyle's War, Midsomer Murders, Space: 1999, and Upstairs, Downstairs, among others.

1956 – SUEZ CRISIS

When the President of Egypt, General Abdel Nasser, nationalized the Suez Canal in 1956, it would be an understatement to say that UK Prime Minister Anthony Eden took it badly. Believing that Nasser had violated a treaty between England, France, and Egypt and could become another fascist dictator, he partnered with British and French armed forces for an invasion of the country to take control of the canal back. The invasion, under the disguise of acting as a peacekeeping force between Egypt and Israel, was roundly condemned by Britain and France's allies all over the world, forcing them to back down.

1958 – MOTORWAY SYSTEM OPENS WITH THE M6

The plan to have a series of high-speed roads throughout the United Kingdom was first thought up during World War II, but the government lacked the power to build roads that were not automatically rights of way until the Special Roads Act 1949. Known as the Preston Bypass when it was built, the M6 was the first official motorway in Britain. It is still the longest in the country at 230 miles from the Midlands to the Scottish border.

1963 – DOCTOR WHO PREMIERES

In November, one of television's longest-running shows materialized when Doctor Who first hit the airwaves. Envisioned by BBC Head of Drama Sydney Newman as a science-fiction series that could teach kids about history, concepts such as The Doctor, the TARDIS, the Daleks, and so on are now part of our pop culture lexicon.

1964 – HAROLD WILSON BECOMES PRIME MINISTER

Harold Wilson won his first time as Prime Minister in the 1964 election that delivered a Labor Majority for the first time since 1951. His domestic policy during his first term in Downing Street focused on social reforms, including workers' rights, civil liberties, housing, healthcare, and education. He was also a strong champion of the United Kingdom, joining the European Community (later known as the European Union). Wilson would end up being the last strong Labour Leader until Tony Blair.

1965 – COMPREHENSIVE EDUCATION SYSTEM ESTABLISHED

It may seem hard to believe even today, but there was a time when the British educational system was even more classist. To alleviate what it saw as social differences caused by the placement system that often left poorer children behind. The Labour government, under Secretary of State for Education Anthony Crossland, implemented a policy to compel all secondary schools in Britain to convert to this system and accept students regardless of academic qualifications or income.

1966 – ENGLAND WINS THE WORLD CUP

When you hear about English football fans saying, "It's coming home," this is the moment that they are referencing. The game of football (or soccer as some Americans call it) was first invented with its current rules in England, and in 1966, England hosted (and won) its first World Cup. This monumental moment in English sports made legends out of the players and is always seen with nostalgia even today.

1967 – ABORTION AND HOMOSEXUALITY PARTIALLY DECRIMINALIZED

Amongst the personal liberties expanded by the British government under Wilson and Labour included a partial decriminalization of abortion and homosexuality via the Abortion Act 1967 and the Sexual Offences Act 1967. The first act legalized the practice for up to 28 weeks on a wide number of grounds, while the latter removed the criminality of sexual acts between two consenting male partners over the age of 21. It was the first volley in the sexual revolution of the 1960s in Britain and helped to increase rights within the country.

1968 – THE TROUBLES BEGIN

Historians disagree on when exactly "The Troubles" began in Northern Ireland, but 1968 saw an increase in activism and violence from both sides that would continue until the Good Friday Agreement in 1998. Catholic activists began protesting for civil rights and found themselves often attacked by loyalist counter-demonstrators and the Royal Ulster Constabulary. Increasing violence would see the IRA come back into formation in 1969, waging a terror campaign throughout Northern Ireland and other parts of the United Kingdom.

1970 – AGE OF MAJORITY LOWERED TO 18

In Britain, the age of majority for males was 21 since the Medieval Period, and they could not inherit property fully or marry of their own free will until that age was attained (for women, it was 14 if married and 16 if single). In 1970, the Labour government concluded that this was incredibly outdated given modern advancements in society and made the age of majority 18 for everyone. In addition to other rights that vested at 18, the government also lowered the voting age.

1971 – DECIMALIZED CURRENCY

Prior to 1971, British currency could be a little confusing for anyone born outside the UK. Each pound was about 240 pence (or pennies), each penny could be broken down into farthings or halfpennies, pence could be twopence, threepence, groats, and sixpence, and a shilling equaled twelve pence. Come Decimal Day on February 15, 1971, Britain switched to 100 pence equaling 1 pound, and left halfpenny and twopence coins in circulation until 1984.

1973 – UNITED KINGDOM JOINS THE EUROPEAN COMMUNITIES

In 1972, Prime Minister Edward Heath signed the Treaty of Accession 1972, which took effect on January 1, 1973, and the United Kingdom joined the European Communities, the precursor of the European Union. The UK would remain a member until the Brexit vote of 2016 and officially broke away from the EU on January 31, 2020. How exactly the break will affect Britain economically remains to be seen.

1977 – QUEEN ELIZABETH II SILVER JUBILEE

1977 marked the 25th year of Queen Elizabeth II's reign, and celebrations took place throughout the year for her Silver Jubilee. In addition to numerous street parties and celebrations in Britain, the Queen opened the Jubilee Walkway and the Southbank Jubilee Gardens. As a side note, Her Majesty's own Jubilee procession led the Sex Pistols

to infamously do one of their own on a boat down the River Thames while playing their new single "God Save the Queen."

1979 – MARGARET THATCHER BECOMES PRIME MINISTER

Margaret Thatcher was the first woman to become Prime Minister in 1979 and presided over the government for over 11 years, making her the seventh-longest premiership in Britain's history. She presided over massive changes to the British government and economy, including the privatization of many of the country's nationalized industries, from telecommunications to transportation. Her legacy is controversial, but you cannot deny the impact she had on British politics – still felt today.

1981 – WEDDING OF PRINCE CHARLES AND LADY DIANA

Watching on television the wedding of Prince Charles and Lady Diana Spencer would have seemed like a fairytale to most. Certainly, the biggest event of the year, Charles and Diana's marriage, would provide drama for years to come until their divorce in 1996. The events that took place before, during, and after continue to shape the monarchy to this day.

1982 – FALKLANDS WAR

The defining military conflict for Britain in the 1980s, the Falklands War, began when Argentina occupied the British dependent territories of the Falkland Islands as well as South Georgia and the Sandwich Islands. Hostilities lasted ten weeks, and the British military response resulted in Argentina's surrender. Interestingly, the war helped to improve life for both the islanders and Argentinians, the former having their British citizenship restored and economy boosted, while the latter saw the military government's image crumble and democracy restored the next year.

1984 – MINERS' STRIKE

Beginning March 6, 1984, the Miners' Strike was a walkout in protest of coalmine (also known as colliery) closures in the UK by Thatcher's Conservative government. The National Union of Mineworkers held out for a year until many returned to work after union pay ran out. This severely reduced the power of the union to negotiate with the government and arguably made the economic situation of the miners worse as customers switched to gas or found other providers.

1985 – LIVE AID

Founded by musicians and philanthropists Bob Geldof and Midge Ure, Live Aid was a benefit concert for famine relief in Ethiopia held simultaneously at JFK Stadium in Philadelphia and Wembley Stadium in London. Acts in London included Adam Ant, Sting, Phil Collins, U2, Dire Straits, David Bowie, The Who, and Queen, amongst others. The concert raised over $127 million for famine relief.

1989 – TIM BERNERS-LEE INVENTS THE WORLD WIDE WEB

Arguably the most significant technological advance of the 20th Century, the worldwide Web (or the Web as we know it today), was the creation of Sir Tim Berners-Lee in 1989. It was the product of Berners-Lee's merger of hypertext with the internet to create an information-sharing network amongst researchers. The first public web pages appeared only four years later and has revolutionized our world.

1990 – POLL TAX AND TACHER'S RESIGNATION

Margaret Thatcher's government introduced the "Community Charge," more commonly known as the Poll Tax, in 1990 as a flat-rate per-capita tax on every adult in the UK to fund local government. To say that the poll tax proved unpopular would be a massive understatement. The unpopularity brought the first serious challenge to Thatcher's leadership of the Conservatives, and she opted to resign, effectively ending her tenure as Prime Minister.

1992 – THE CHANNEL TUNNEL OPENS

Also known as the Eurotunnel or the Chunnel, the Channel Tunnel is an underground tunnel below the English Channel. Opened in 1992, it has been a vital link for trade of goods between the UK and Continental Europe as well as a major player in passenger travel.

1993 – FIRST PREMIER LEAGUE CHAMPIONSHIP

After 1991, 22 top-tier football teams resigned from the Football League to set up their own commercially-independent league, the Premier League. The Premier League became the highest tier of English football, and the 1992-1993 season ended with Manchester United finishing ten points ahead of Aston Villa to secure the league's first championship. The Premier League's success has kept it a driving force in football today and may have partially inspired the ill-conceived European Super League.

1994 – FIRST WOMEN PRIESTS ORDAINED IN THE CHURCH OF ENGLAND

March 12, 1994, saw the ordination of thirty-two women as priests into the Church of England. While previous branches of the Anglican and Episcopalian Churches had ordained women in the past, it was not permitted in the Church of England until the General Synod passed the measure in 1992. By 2004, one in five priests in the Anglican Church was a woman.

1995 – BSE OUTBREAK

One of the worst virus outbreaks in Britain until COVID-19, Bovine spongiform encephalopathy (more popularly known as "Mad Cow Disease"), was a neurodegenerative disease that struck cattle. The virus had been identified as early as 1984 but experienced an alarming surge in 1995, with the United Kingdom experiencing 14,562 cases. It was also discovered during this time that a variant of the virus could be passed to humans by eating BSE-tainted meat.

1997 – NEW LABOUR

As the Conservative Party slid further under the premiership of John Major, Tony Blair took charge of Labour's leadership and formed a more center-left coalition that was dubbed "New Labour." The results were striking as Blair's Labour Party won 145 new seats in the 1997 General Election and reduced the Tories to a mere 165 seats to Labour's 418. The Labour government would last for the next thirteen years until the Conservative-Liberal Democrat coalition in 2010.

1997 - AUGUST - DIANA, PRINCESS OF WALES, DIES IN A CAR CRASH IN PARIS

Diana was the ex-wife of the heir to the British throne, Charles, Prince of Wales. A controversial figure in life, Diana's death in a car crash in Paris provoked widespread public mourning. On September 6, one million people lined the streets of London for her funeral. It was later discovered that the driver of the car in which he, Diana, and her friend Dodi Al Fayed were killed had more than the legal limit of alcohol in his blood and was traveling at over 100mph.

1997 - HONG KONG RETURNED TO CHINA

In the 1980s, Margaret Thatcher agreed to return Hong Kong to China in 1997. So, like clockwork, in 1997, Britain handed Hong Kong back to China, ending more than 150 years of British rule. This is considered the 'final' nail in the coffin of the former British Empire (though Britain continues to have a few former imperial colonies under its rule, none are large or as important as Hong Kong was).

1998 – GOOD FRIDAY AGREEMENT

Also known as the Belfast Agreement, the Good Friday Agreement finally put an end to violence in Northern Ireland by giving the country a greater say over its affairs through devolved government and demilitarization. Voters in Northern Ireland accepted the agreement in a referendum on May 22 by an overwhelming majority of 71%.

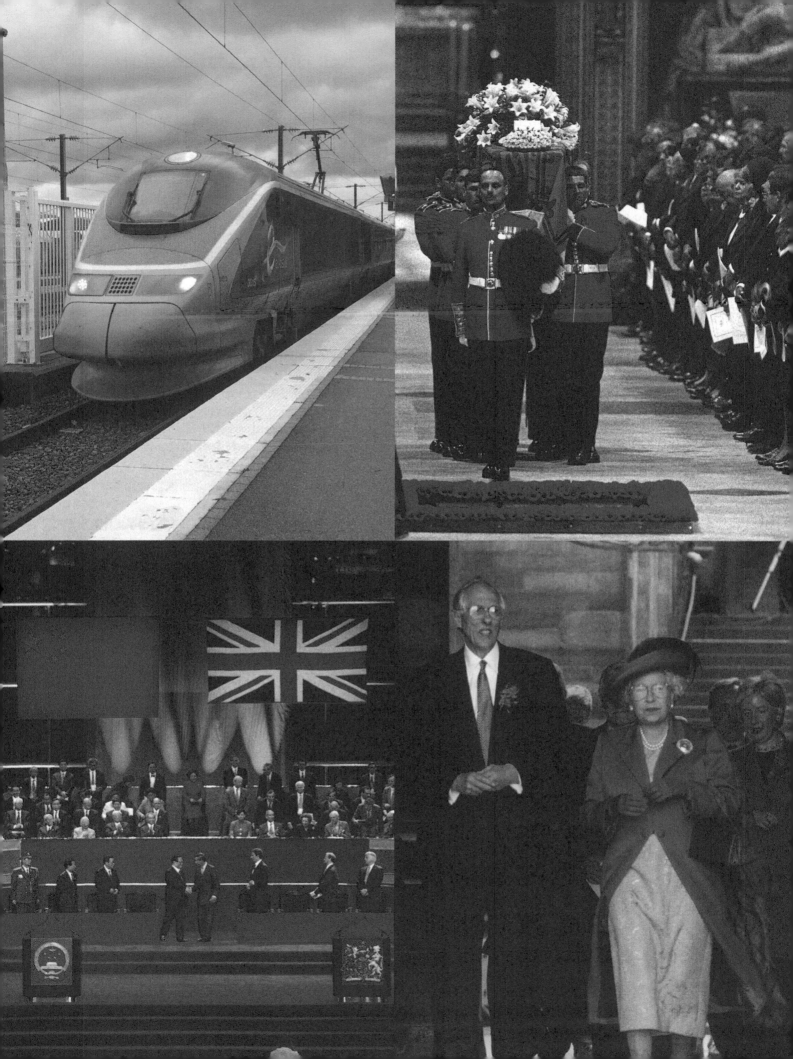

1999 – WELSH PARLIAMENT AND SCOTTISH PARLIAMENT OPEN

Northern Ireland wasn't the only beneficiary of government devolution in the 1990s. The Labour government also helped to form and give power to the Senedd Cymru (the Welsh Parliament) as well as the Scottish Parliament. Both institutions continue to have power over the internal affairs in Wales and Scotland to this day.

2000 – NEW MILLENNIUM

All across the world, the coming of the year 2000 brought both excitement and apprehension. While some worried about the possibility of a "Y2K" bug shutting down computers, Britain prepared for the coming of the new millennium with the construction of the Millennium Dome and the London Eye. While the Dome initially failed, it was later reinvented as the O2 Arena, while the Eye continues to be a popular attraction for the city.

2001 - FOOT-AND-MOUTH DISEASE WREAKS HAVOC ON RURAL BRITAIN

The nine-month epidemic of 'foot-and-mouth' disease resulted in the culling of millions of animals and devastated large sections of the rural economy. The crisis brought the countryside to a virtual standstill, and the cost to British farming was put between £800 million and £2.4 billion. The Labour government was heavily criticized for its handling of the crisis.

2005 - CHARLES MARRIES CAMILLA, FINALLY

After a long negotiation, the Queen finally consented to Charles Marrying Camilla in a special non-Royal ceremony. It's the first time a divorced heir to the throne and a divorced woman have been allowed to marry within the Royal Family (and a situation that in the 1930s caused a massive crisis). A symbolic event that showed how the Royal Family had been forced to change with the times. It was announced in 2022 that the Queen would like Camilla to actually become Queen when Charles accedes to the throne.

2005 - JULY 7, 2005 LONDON BOMBINGS

The first post-9/11 terrorist attack in London was big in scope and massive in its carnage. Dozens were killed when Islamic Fundamentalist terrorists attacked London's transport network. Three terrorists separately detonated three homemade bombs in quick succession aboard London Underground trains across the city and, later, a fourth terrorist detonated another bomb on a double-decker bus in Tavistock Square. Londoners adopted a 'London can take it' blitz mentality and didn't let the event materially change life in London.

2005 JULY 28 - IRISH REPUBLICAN ARMY (IRA) ANNOUNCES A FORMAL END TO ITS ARMED CAMPAIGN

In the wake of the 1999 Good Friday Agreement, peace came to Northern Ireland, and finally, in 2005, the IRA finally laid down its arms, ending decades of fear and terror on Britain's mainland.

2008 FINANCIAL CRISIS STARTS WITH NORTHERN ROCK

A little-known bank in Britain ran into liquidity troubles that then ricocheted throughout the financial system, eventually leading to the financial crash in 2008 that led to recession and fundamental changes in the world's financial system. We are still dealing with the effect to this day.

2011 - APRIL - PRINCE WILLIAM MARRIES KATHERINE MIDDLETON

On a beautiful spring day, Prince William Married Katherine Middleton, a commoner. It was said the wedding was watched by 1 billion people all over the world. The wedding, and the child born the next year, ushered in the new generation of the Royal Family, assuring stability to the family line for decades to come. It's said Will & Kate are probably the most popular Royals after the Queen.

2012 - LONDON HOSTS SUMMER WINTER OLYMPICS

While the Diamond Jubilee was also celebrated in

2012, the summer ended with London hosting the Olympic Games in suitably grand fashion. Even the Queen joined in by appearing on screen with James Bond. After years of preparation, London hosted what many consider to be the 'best' games so far in the 21st Century.

2014 - SCOTTISH INDEPENDENCE REFERENDUM

The Kingdom held. Scottish Nationalists have campaigned for years for Scotland to gain its Independence from the United Kingdom, and they got their chance to vote for it in a referendum in 2016. However, a majority of Scots opted to stay in the Kingdom and put to rest the question of Scottish Independence for a generation, though the Scottish Nationalist Party continues to campaign for Independence.

2016 - BREXIT REFERENDUM

It seemed like the 2010s were destined to become the decade of referendums. In 2016, campaigners to leave the European Union finally got their wish, and it was put to a vote amongst the British public. And in a shock result, a majority of Britain voted to leave the European Union, unleashing years of political squabbling, deadlock, and economic uncertainty for Britain.

2021 - PRINCE PHILIP DIES

After a short illness, Prince Philip died at the height of the COVID-19 pandemic. As a result, he did not have a grand state funeral but a much more subdued affair which under COVID guidelines saw HM The Queen sitting by herself at the funeral. The very same day, staffers at Number 10 Downing Street were having a party, which would later lead to a political crisis in 2022 for Boris Johnson that, as of this writing, is still unfolding.

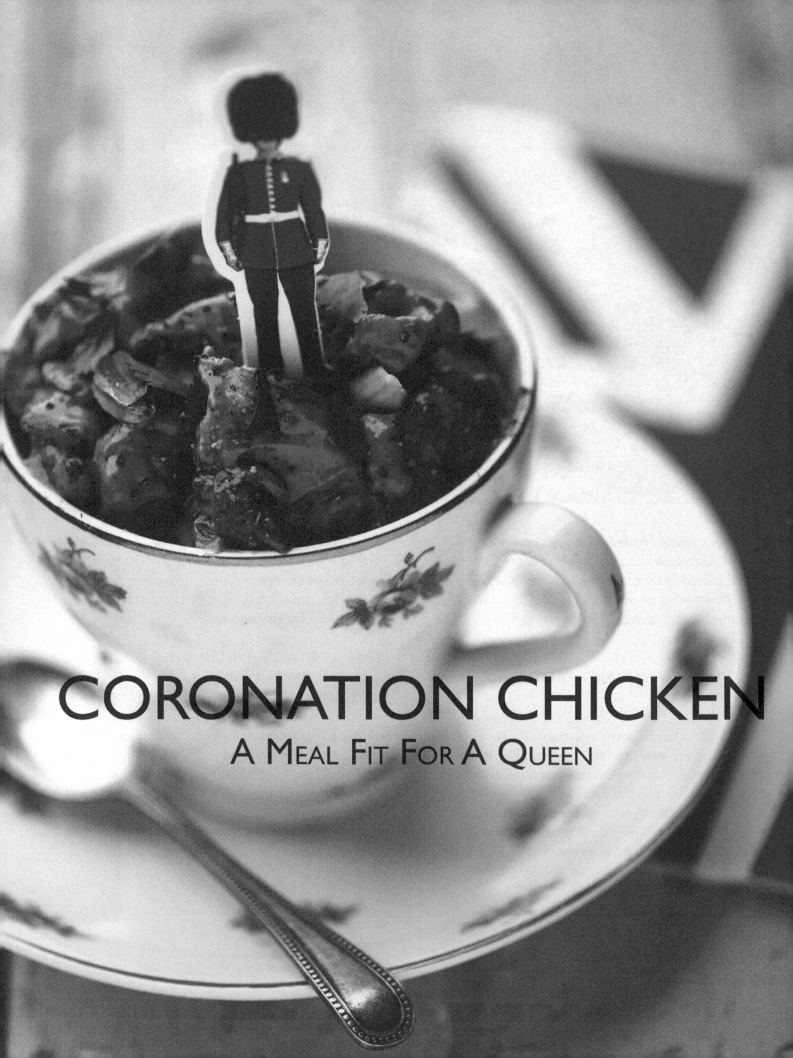

CORONATION CHICKEN
A MEAL FIT FOR A QUEEN

Coronation chicken is a combination of cold-cooked chicken meat, herbs and spices, and a creamy mayonnaise-based sauce. It can be eaten as a salad or used to fill sandwiches. It was developed in celebration of the Queen's Coronation in 1953 and has been served at events since then in celebration.

Normally bright yellow, coronation chicken is usually flavored with curry powder or paste, although more sophisticated versions of the recipe are made using fresh herbs and spices and additional ingredients such as flaked almonds, raisins, and crème fraîche. The original dish calls for dried apricot and not raisins and uses curry powder instead of Indian curry paste made from scratch, as fresh Indian curry spices were almost unobtainable in post-war Britain.

Constance Spry, an English food writer and flower arranger, and Rosemary Hume, a chef, both principals of the Cordon Bleu Cookery School in London, are credited with the invention of coronation chicken. Preparing the food for the banquet of the coronation of Queen Elizabeth II in 1953, Spry proposed the recipe of cold chicken, curry cream sauce, and dressing that would later become known as coronation chicken.

Coronation chicken may have been inspired by jubilee chicken, a dish prepared for the silver jubilee of George V in 1935, which mixed chicken with Mayonnaise and curry. Additionally, for the Queen's Golden Jubilee in 2002, another celebratory dish was devised, also called Jubilee chicken.

Here's the recipe to make yourself.

Ingredients:

For the chicken

- 2 Roasting chickens
- 1 Carrot
- 1 Bouquet garni
- Water
- White wine (a splash)
- A pinch of salt
- 4 Peppercorns

For the sauce

- 2oz Onion (chopped)
- 2tsp Curry powder
- 1tsp Tomato purée
- 1 Red wine
- Water
- 1 Bay leaf
- Lemon
- Lemon juice
- 3tbsp Apricot purée, or apricot jam
- ¾pint Mayonnaise
- 3tbsp Whipped cream, plus a little more
- 1tbsp Oil
- Salt and pepper
- A pinch of Sugar

Here are the directions based on the original recipe from 1953.

1. Remove the skin and any bones from the chicken and cut it into small pieces.
2. Heat up the vegetable oil in a medium saucepan and add the 0nion. Cook on medium heat for about 3 minutes until the onion is soft and translucent.
3. Add the curry paste, tomato puree, red wine, bay leaf, and the lemon juice to the cooked onions.
4. Lower the heat and simmer uncovered for about 10 minutes until reduced. Remove the bay leaf and leave to onion sauce to cool.
5. Finely chop the apricot halves and puree them through a sieve or with a handheld blender.
6. Place the pureed apricots into a bowl and mix in the Mayonnaise.
7. Add the onion sauce and apricot jam and mix well.
8. Whip the cream to stiff peaks and fold this also into the mixture. Mix well.
9. Season with salt & pepper, and if necessary, add a little extra Lemon Juice.
10. Finally, fold in the chicken pieces coating them with the mixture well.
11. Garnish with watercress and serve.
12. Serves 4 to 6 as a salad with additional salad ingredients or makes eight rounds of sandwiches. Also wonderful as a vol au vent or pie filling.

70 FACTS FOR 70 YEARS

In celebration of the Queen's Platinum Jubilee - seventy years on the throne - we've compiled seventy interesting facts and figures about her life and reign that summarize how important she is to Britain, and the world!

1. The Queen's Parents are King George VI and Queen Elizabeth, the Queen Mother

2. The Queen was born on April 21, 1926

3. She was born at 17 Bruton St in Mayfair (not in a hospital). It's now a hotel and restaurant.

4. Due to tradition, the Home Secretary was present in the next room to ensure her 'legitimacy.'

5. When Princess Elizabeth was born, her parents were not the King & Queen and had no prospect of being so. Elizabeth was never meant to be Queen.

6. Her close family called her Lillibet - and that's what she called herself in early letters as well.

7. The Abdication Crisis of Edward VIII led to his brother, Bertie, becoming King George VI and Princess Elizabeth becoming the next Heir to the throne.

8. It was not a sure thing Elizabeth would be the Heir - her parents were still of childbearing age when George VI ascended the throne.

9. Princess Elizabeth never attended formal schooling - she had a governess and was taught everything she 'needed to know' to be a Princess (and later Queen).

10. Despite the lack of formal schooling, Queen Mary thought it important that she learn history (and this was a controversial notion).

11. Growing up, the family lived at 145 Piccadilly but moved to Buckingham Palace when George VI became King.

12. The people of Wales gifted Elizabeth a 'Wendy House' - a 2/3 scale Welsh cottage that became her favorite place to play (they would even lay out tea). It was recently restored.

13. The Queen had her own special troupe of Girl Guides (basically the Girl Scouts) made up of other aristocratic girls. Margaret was a Brownie.

14. During World War II, Elizabeth and Margaret lived at Windsor Castle with their governess and a special detachment of guards (King and Queen stayed in London).

15. Before becoming Queen, Elizabeth and Philip lived at Clarence House (now the official London home of Prince Charles).

16. Her last name is Windsor, and this is the name passed to her children (much to Prince Philip's annoyance).

17. Elizabeth and Philip met when Elizabeth was 13 years old, and Philip was 18 (and serving in the Navy). Obviously, there was not a romance until she was older, but Elizabeth was smitten.

18. Elizabeth attended the coronation of her father, a very rare event in Royal History.

19. Elizabeth spent large parts of her childhood without her parents, who were often on Royal Tours. She was left in the care of a governess.

20. There was a lot of controversy around her marrying Philip as he was foreign (and Heir to a foreign throne), but he was naturalized as British, and everyone seems to be OK with it now.

21. Elizabeth only gave two speeches during World War II - the King didn't like using her for political purposes.

22. During World War II, the King insisted that the family follow all the rationing laws just the same as everyone else. Their diet was supplemented with game from the Royal Estates and food they grew in their own Victory Garden at Windsor Castle.

23. Despite no formal schooling, she also received private tutoring from eminent

teachers at Eton College (a boys-only school).

24. Towards the end of the war, Princess Elizabeth served in the Auxiliary Territorial Service. She trained as a driver and mechanic.

25. She became Queen on February 6, 1952, on the death of her father. She was just 25 years old.

26. She was not in the United Kingdom when George VI died, she was on an official visit to Kenya, and it was several hours before she knew she was now Queen.

27. Margaret and Elizabeth would often put on plays for family and sometimes residents of Windsor to raise money for charity during the war.

28. Sourcing her wedding dress proved difficult as, after World War II, rationing was still in effect. Many women sent in their clothing coupons to help her (but it was actually illegal to transfer ration coupons, so they were returned).

29. Princess Elizabeth married Prince Philip in 1947.

30. Elizabeth and Philip's wedding was one of the first to be public - previous Royal Weddings happened behind closed doors.

31. She has been quoted more than once in regard to her duty, saying, "I have to be seen to be believed."

32. She knows how to drive but does not have a license because they are issued in her name.

33. HM The Queen also doesn't have a passport - all passports are issued in her name.

34. The Queen has four children - Prince Charles (the Heir to the throne), Princess Anne, Prince Andrew, and Prince Edward.

35. Her mother, Queen Elizabeth, lived to be 101

36. She cannot vote.

37. She cannot hold a political opinion - the Monarchy is apolitical.

38. She cannot set foot in the House of Commons (the last King to do so - Charles I - lost his head).

39. She used to be exempt from paying taxes, but after various controversies, she agreed to pay tax on her personal income.

40. Her first prime minister was Sir Winston Churchill

41. On the night of VE day (and the next night), Princess Elizabeth and Princess Margaret were allowed (albeit escorted) to celebrate in the streets with the crowds.

42. The official residence is Buckingham Palace (though the official court is at St James), and it's where she receives official visitors.

43. While the Queen is Elizabeth II in England, in Scotland, she's technically Elizabeth I because Scotland wasn't united with England during the reign of Elizabeth I.

44. There have been 12 US presidents on her watch.

45. She has received over 3 million letters, cards, and postcards since she began her reign.

46. There are 775 rooms in Buckingham Palace, her official London residence.

47. She is the head of state of 15 countries.

48. While she is the ceremonial head of state, a Governor-General handles the day-to-day 'Queening.'

49. She is a patron of over 600 charities.

50. The Queen has the right to approve or disapprove marriages for the first six people in line of the throne (it used to be more, but it was changed in 2011).

51. She is the head of the Church of England - founded by Henry VIII.

52. She also takes an oath to preserve the Church of Scotland (which is a different Christian denomination).

53. Her coronation was the first to be televised, and there was a great debate as to whether or not such a thing would be appropriate. The compromise was that some bits were not televised, but most of it was.

54. The Queen does not have to curtsy to anyone. Her family must, in theory, curtsy to her, but she has exempted close family members from having to do this.

55. 1992 was, as the Queen has said, her /Annus horribilis/. It was the year Windsor Castle burned down; Princess Anne Divorced her husband, Charles and Diana separated, among other things.

56. The Channel Islands are not part of the United Kingdom, but the Queen is their Monarch. The islands used to be part of the Duchy of Normandy, which no longer exists. When they toast the Queen, they say, "Our Queen, The Duke."

57. She does not have to stand for God Save the Queen since it's about her.

58. Her wedding dress was decorated with 10,000 pearls and had a 13-foot train.

59. Speaking of trains, The Queen has her own train and carriages but more often than not now will take a regular passenger train.

60. She does not have her own 'Queen Force One' and flies on specially chartered planes (or planes provided by the Royal Air Force). She does have use of a helicopter, however.

61. The Queen has a personal net worth of over $500 million. Income comes from her private estates and the Sovereign Grant (funds provided by the government to fund her official duties).

62. Eight thousand people attended her Coronation at Westminster Abbey.

63. The Queen's current car is a specially made 2002 Bentley Limousine. It cost $10 million, which is why it hasn't been replaced.

64. The Crown Estate has a portfolio worth around £10 billion, but the Queen does not control this and cannot sell any part of it - it's held in trust by the nation. However, she does own personal property that's not part of the Crown Estate.

65. The Queen's birthday is April 21. Her 'official' birthday is celebrated in June with the Trooping the Colour ceremony (because the weather is usually better).

66. Her full title as Queen is "Her Majesty Elizabeth the Second, by the Grace of God of the United Kingdom of Great Britain and Northern Ireland, and of Her other Realms and Territories Queen, Head of the Commonwealth, Defender of the Faith."

67. The Queen technically owns all the Mute Swans in England (they're counted every year in a special ceremony called swan upping).

68. She sends a special card to subjects who have reached 100 years old. She's sent over 100,000 during her reign. One wonders if she will be sending a card to herself in a few years!

69. She's the first Monarch to circumnavigate the globe. She did it on a six-month tour on her former yacht Britannia.

70. The Queen is the longest-reigning Monarch in British history, having surpassed Queen Victoria. Long may she reign!

THE JUBILEE YEARS

TWILIGHT OF THE SECOND ELIZABETHAN AGE

The Queen Mother, more affectionately known as the Queen Mum, celebrated her 100th birthday in 2000, going on to live almost another two years. Her birthday celebrations were a raging success—everybody loved her. When King George VI died in 1952, Winston Churchill encouraged the new widow Elizabeth not to fade from sight but to be the warm, generous spirit the country was used to seeing. So she did just that, remaining in the spotlight at events and acting as a kind of grandmotherly influence on the country, as well as a constant source of advice and companionship for her daughter, the Queen. But with her death in 2002, Queen Elizabeth became the new grandmother of the nation.

Elizabeth had celebrated her Silver Jubilee in 1977, 25 years on the throne, amid strife in Ireland (it was just two years later that her beloved Uncle Dickie was blown up on his yacht with other members of his family, off the coast of Ireland), and a rising tide of bad press for the family with Diana's media circus coming to a head in the 90s and Charles giving interviews to slight his parents, along with the Queen's Annus Horribilis in 1992. Elizabeth had survived an assassination attempt in 1981 when a gunman took a few shots at her while she was on horseback during the Trooping of the Colour—causing one newspaper to actually compliment her, "Her Majesty showed guts, courage, pluck, bravery, and bottle." Even while she was taking her hits in the press during the 80s and 90s, she was also racking up some goodwill among her people. By 1997 when Elizabeth and Philip celebrated their 50th wedding anniversary, things were looking up for the Queen. She was a grandma, Philip and Charles were working together on renovations of Windsor Castle (an unlikely but beneficial alliance), the Queen was paying taxes (which pleased the press and public to no end), and the Palace was paying more attention to public opinion polls about the royal family. The Queen's image was softening.

2002 was the Queen's Golden Jubilee year, marking 50 years on the throne. The year started out a little dicey, first with the death of Princess Margaret followed six weeks later by the death of the Queen Mum. The Queen Mother's funeral was a surprisingly huge event, with crowds of people lined up to view her coffin. It had been a hard start to the year, and Queen Elizabeth was more willing to show her emotions to the public than she ever had before. She became the "senior royal lady" at age 75 and seemed to shake off the gloom, as much as was possible, in time for the privately-funded Jubilee celebrations that summer (privately funded except for the security costs that came out of the government's wallet).

Golden Jubilee celebrations lasted three months. The Queen took another royal tour, opening the Commonwealth Games, visiting Northern Ireland, and touring around Great Britain, covering 3500 miles in the royal train and visiting 70 cities. She visited a Sikh temple, a Hindu temple, a Jewish museum, and a mosque. She lit a bonfire at the Victoria Memorial outside Buckingham Palace—one of 2000 bonfires lit at the same time, including one at Treetops in Kenya where she had been staying when she heard the news that she was the new Queen. She told the country, "[It is] my resolve to continue, with the support of my family, to serve the people of this great nation of ours to the best of my ability through the changing times ahead."

The parties in London lasted four days, with two huge concerts in the gardens at Buckingham Palace. Brian May, the guitarist from Queen, played the national anthem from the roof of the Palace, Eric Clapton played "Layla," Paul McCartney played "Hey Jude." The Queen might not have known who all the performers were—she asked Eric Clapton if he was any good on the guitar—but she put in her earplugs and showed up at the celebrations. For the Jubilee service at St. Paul's, she rode down The Mall in the Gold State Coach and enjoyed a flyover by the RAF Red Arrows afterward. The Palace was pleasantly surprised with the popularity of the events. A former Palace secretary, Charles Anson, commented, "People woke up and realized that Her Majesty was about stability, serenity, continuity, calm through adversity, and humor when things are going wrong. Suddenly they got the point of the Queen, who had been doing her job for fifty years."

After the success of the Golden Jubilee year, the Queen kept swimming along with just a few changes to her routine. She started riding smaller horses (in her 70s, most of us wouldn't be riding at all), she spent more time with her grandchildren, she allowed Charles and Camilla to marry in a civil ceremony, she posed for photos with Annie Leibovitz. The movie The Queen also came out in 2006, rocketing Her Majesty's popularity again. While Elizabeth refused to see it, she did invite the actress playing her, Helen Mirren, to join her for tea in her box at Ascot. Helen Mirren remarked, "I wouldn't have been invited to tea if she had hated the film." Elizabeth also continued making friends around the globe, hosting a dinner for the Bushes at the British Embassy in Washington in 2007, making a joke at her own expense: "I wondered whether I should start this toast by saying, 'When I was here in 1776,' but I don't think I will."

2012 was the year of the Queen's Diamond Jubilee—60 years on the throne and the year that London hosted the Summer Olympics. Queen Victoria was the only other monarch to make it to 60 years on the throne. This time instead of a royal tour of the Commonwealth, Elizabeth and Philip stuck to the United Kingdom, sending their children and grandchildren around the world in their place. For the celebrations in London, the royal couple took part in the largest flotilla on the Thames in history. One thousand boats spread out for seven-and-a-half miles, with the Queen and Philip waving to crowds of over a million people lining the riverbanks. They both suffered from the exhaustion and exposure of it afterward (it was cold and rainy), but Elizabeth didn't think it was right to deprive her people of the spectacle they were looking for. This was also just after The King's Speech was released, a movie she chose to see. She loved it, feeling that it showed the dedication, integrity, and courage of her parents. After her Jubilee service and the royal flyover this time, she waved to the crowds and commented, "Incredible people; bless them!" Simon Shama, the great British historian, and author, noted that "there is something simple and innocent . . . which people respect enormously in the Queen."

The Opening Ceremonies of the Summer Olympics really demonstrated her willingness to take part in her own popularity. Danny Boyle, the director of the video clip to open the Olympics, wanted a way to introduce the monarch to the world. He wrote to the Palace and told them his plan and asked if it would be ok if they used

an actor to portray the Queen. The Palace reply was a closely-guarded secret and shocked him enormously: "we're delighted for you to do it, and Her Majesty would like to be in it herself." She wasn't supposed to have any lines but inserted the "Good evening, Mr. Bond" herself and let her dogs be filmed, as well. While Daniel Craig was said to be in a grumpy mood the day of filming— who could tell with his perpetual smolder?—the Queen looks positively delighted in the video. Her children and grandchildren didn't even know she was going to make an appearance in the video; they laughed harder than anyone, especially when she jumped out of the helicopter and parachuted into the stadium with Daniel Craig (ok, that part was an actor).

With the end of the Civil List in 2013 (revising the Queen's allowance from Parliament), Charles's popularity increasing, the incredibly photogenic William and Katherine and their children, the engagement of Harry and the American Meghan Markle, the view of the monarchy continues to rise. Harry says of the Queen, "Behind closed doors, she's our grandmother; it's as simple as that." And William says, "She's an incredible role model." The Queen has become a fixture in the lives of millions of British people and people around the world--her purse, her hats, her hairstyle that hasn't changed in fifty years, the way she's always surrounded by her dogs and her family. She has proven not just her dedication and loyalty to the country but her sympathy and compassion for her people. Helen Mirren, her actor-counterpart, said of her, "To be that consistent for that long is amazingly comforting. It shows such reliability. She has never lurched in one direction or another. It is self-discipline, which I think comes from within rather than imposed from outside." And Prime Minister Tony Blair paid her an enduring compliment at a luncheon full of dignitaries and commoners alike, calling her "a symbol of unity in a world of insecurity where nothing stays the same. You are our Queen. We respect and cherish you. You are, simply, the Best of British."

ROYAL WORDS
ROYALS WORDS TO KNOW

As with all things that have been around for a while, the Royal Family has its own set of words and vernacular that may seem incomprehensible to outsiders. Here's a summary of the most important Royal Words so you aren't scratching your head during the next major Royal event!

The Crown - The Crown is an abstract concept that summarizes the entire British State. It is both a person, thing, and legal framework. The Crown is the fount of all authority in Britain, and it is immortal - it never dies.

Queen Consort - The wife of a King - a Queen that does not 'reign.'

Peerage - A legal system historically comprising various hereditary titles (and sometimes non-hereditary titles) composed of assorted noble ranks such as Duke, Earl, Marquess, Lord, etc.

Honour - A system of awards to people in Britain who achieve great, important, or charitable things. The most famous 'honour' is a Knighthood or Damehood, which allows someone to address as Sir or Dame.

HRH - His Royal Highness/Her Royal Highness - A special Royal Title available only to the Children of the Monarch and their spouses.

HM - Her Majesty, His Majesty - The abbreviation of the formal address that someone is expected to make to the reigning Monarch.

Buck House - A colloquial term for Buckingham Palace.

Interregnum - The period between reigning monarchs. The most famous one is the Interregnum period when Oliver Cromwell ruled Britain.

Sovereign - The word sovereign is frequently used synonymously with Monarch. There are numerous titles in a monarchical rule which can belong to the sovereign. The sovereign is the autonomous head of the state and the source of all governmental authority.

Royal Household - The rather large staff of people who run the admin part of the Royal family - the Queen's events, affairs, etc., along with other minor Royals. It's a mini-government in its own right, with its own rules and traditions (some of which are not always clear to outsiders).

Heir Apparent - An heir apparent is a person who is first in order of succession and cannot be displaced from inheriting by the birth of another person. Prince Charles is the current Heir Apparent.

Heir Presumptive - A person who is first in order of succession but can be displaced by the birth of a more eligible heir is known as heir presumptive

Accession - When a monarch's reign begins, which in the British tradition is immediately upon the death of the previous Monarch.

Abdication - The act by which a monarch 'resigns' from the throne and ceases to be Monarch - usually requires an act of parliament to enact (and in the British Monarch's case, an act in all Commonwealth realms as well). The last to abdicate was Edward VIII.

Privy Purse - The Privy Purse is the British sovereign's private income. It used to also include the money provided by the British government to fund the Royal Family. It was replaced by the...

Sovereign Grant - The money provided to the Royal Family to fulfill its constitutional duties. It currently comes from a percentage of revenue derived from the Crown Estate and does not come from general taxation.

Crown Estate - The vast portfolio of property that used to be in the personal ownership of the reigning Monarch but is not in possession by the state and operated for the benefit of the British people (and of which a portion is provided to the Royal Family to fund its activities).

Made in the USA
Coppell, TX
03 June 2022